Especially for

....

From

....

Date

....

THE BIBLE PROMISE BOOK®

for the

Overwhelmed Heart

THE BIBLE PROMISE BOOK®

for the Overwhelmed Heart

Written and Compiled by
JANICE THOMPSON

BARBOUR BOOKS
An Imprint of Barbour Publishing, Inc.

Print ISBN 978-1-63409-223-4

eBook Editions:
Adobe Digital Edition (.epub) 978-1-63409-844-1
Kindle and MobiPocket Edition (.prc) 978-1-63409-845-8

Published by Barbour Books, an imprint of Barbour Publishing, Inc., P.O. Box 719, Uhrichsville, Ohio 44683, www.barbourbooks.com

Our mission is to publish and distribute inspirational products offering exceptional value and biblical encouragement to the masses.

Printed in China.

INTRODUCTION

Whatever you happen to be going through, no matter how overwhelmed you might be, answers to life's most difficult questions can be found in the Word of God. Searching them out is key. The Bible speaks to every situation, even the most hopeless one. Check out this verse from Psalm 61:2 (TLB): "For wherever I am, though far away at the ends of the earth, I will cry to you for help. When my heart is faint and overwhelmed, lead me to the mighty, towering Rock of safety." God is our Rock and His Word is our guide book to surviving. . .and thriving.

This collection of Bible verses, prayers, and hymn lyrics will encourage you when you're feeling down and bring comfort when you're struggling. Each section opens with a prayer written for a specific topic and closes with praises from a relevant hymn. It is in no way intended to replace regular Bible study or the use of a concordance for in-depth study of a subject. There are many facets of your life and many topics in the Bible that are not covered here.

But, for example, if you are feeling extremely overwhelmed with the busyness of life, some of the Bible's wisdom and comfort is available to you here under the topic of "Busyness." If you're in need of comfort, there's a section for that, too. All topics are arranged alphabetically for ease of use.

It's time to get beyond the feelings of being overwhelmed and find rest—true rest—in your Lord and Savior. What are you waiting for? Let's dive in and see what He has for us.

CONTENTS

Acceptance

Father, what a wonderful word acceptance is. I accepted your Son as my Lord and Savior. I accept the wonderful gifts You lavish on me, and I accept Your joy in place of sorrow. May others around me come to know You and accept Your plan for their lives, too. May I be a witness to Your goodness. Amen.

"Very truly I tell you, whoever accepts anyone I send accepts me; and whoever accepts me accepts the one who sent me."

JOHN 13:20 NIV

"And I will ask the Father, and he will give you another advocate to help you and be with you forever—the Spirit of truth. The world cannot accept him, because it neither sees him nor knows him. But you know him, for he lives with you and will be in you."

JOHN 14:16–17 NIV

"For I gave them the words you gave me and they accepted them. They knew with certainty that I came from you, and they believed that you sent me."

JOHN 17:8 NIV

"Later, when I returned to Jerusalem, I was praying in the Temple, and I saw a vision. I saw the Lord saying to me, 'Hurry! Leave Jerusalem now! The people here will not accept the truth about me.'"

ACTS 22:17–18 NCV

Accept one another, then, just as Christ accepted you, in order to bring praise to God.

ROMANS 15:7 NIV

The person without the Spirit does not accept the things that come from the Spirit of God but considers them foolishness, and cannot understand them because they are discerned only through the Spirit.

1 CORINTHIANS 2:14 NIV

Here is a trustworthy saying that deserves full acceptance: Christ Jesus came into the world to save sinners—of whom I am the worst.

1 TIMOTHY 1:15 NIV

"The Lord disciplines those he loves, and he punishes everyone he accepts as his child."

HEBREWS 12:6 NCV

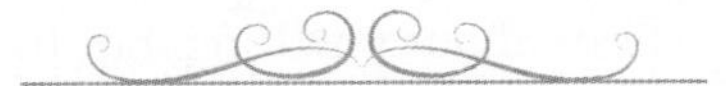

Be still, my soul; the Lord is on thy side;
Bear patiently the cross of grief or pain;
Leave to thy God to order and provide;
In every change He faithful will remain.
Be still, my soul; thy best, thy heavenly Friend
Through thorny ways leads to a joyful end.

"BE STILL, MY SOUL," KATHARINA VON SCHLEGEL

Anxiety

I don't mean to be anxious, Lord. I try so hard to lay down my worries. Maybe that's the problem. . .I'm trying so hard to do it all when I need to be resting in You. Please show me how to fully rest in You so that my heart—so often overwhelmed—can be at rest. Thank You, Father.

Do not be anxious about anything, but in everything by prayer and supplication with thanksgiving let your requests be made known to God. And the peace of God, which surpasses all understanding, will guard your hearts and your minds in Christ Jesus.

PHILIPPIANS 4:6–7 ESV

"Can any one of you by worrying add a single hour to your life?"

MATTHEW 6:27 NIV

Humble yourselves, therefore, under the mighty hand of God so that at the proper time he may exalt you, casting all your anxieties on him, because he cares for you.

1 PETER 5:6–7 ESV

In vain you rise early and stay up late, toiling for food to eat—for he grants sleep to those he loves.

Psalm 127:2 NIV

Search me, O God, and know my heart;
try me and know my anxious thoughts.

Psalm 139:23 NASB

"So do not worry, saying, 'What shall we eat?' or 'What shall we drink?' or 'What shall we wear?'"

Matthew 6:31 NIV

But the Lord answered her, "Martha, Martha, you are anxious and troubled about many things."

Luke 10:41 ESV

So refuse to worry, and keep your body healthy.
But remember that youth,
with a whole life before you, is meaningless.

Ecclesiastes 11:10 NLT

"And why do you worry about clothes? See how the flowers of the field grow. They do not labor or spin."

MATTHEW 6:28 NIV

Don't get angry. Don't be upset; it only leads to trouble.

PSALM 37:8 NCV

"Therefore do not worry about tomorrow, for tomorrow will worry about itself. Each day has enough trouble of its own."

MATTHEW 6:34 NIV

Wait and trust the LORD. Don't be upset when others get rich or when someone else's plans succeed.

PSALM 37:7 NCV

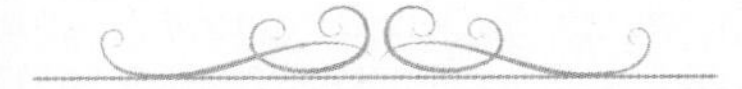

What a fellowship, what a joy divine,
Leaning on the everlasting arms;
What a blessedness, what a peace is mine,
Leaning on the everlasting arms.

Leaning, leaning,
Safe and secure from all alarms;
Leaning, leaning,
Leaning on the everlasting arms.

"Leaning on the Everlasting Arms," Elisha A. Hoffman

Attitude

My attitude determines my altitude. I've heard this so many times, Lord. Sometimes it's hard to keep a positive, upbeat attitude when things around me are spinning out of control or when others aren't behaving as I think they should. That's why I need You so much! Please keep me even-keeled, Father. I need Your help. Amen.

In your relationships with one another,
have the same mindset as Christ Jesus.
PHILIPPIANS 2:5 NIV

Our God is a God who strengthens and encourages you. May he give you the same attitude toward one another that Christ Jesus had.
ROMANS 15:5 NIRV

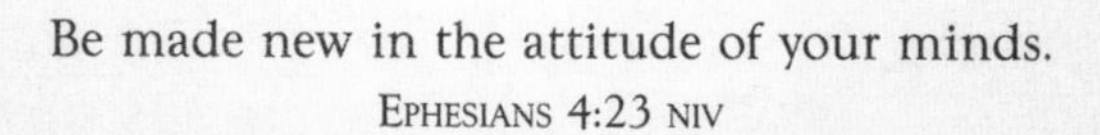

Be made new in the attitude of your minds.
EPHESIANS 4:23 NIV

For the word of God is alive and active. Sharper than any double-edged sword, it penetrates even to dividing soul and spirit, joints and marrow; it judges the thoughts and attitudes of the heart.

HEBREWS 4:12 NIV

Therefore, since Christ suffered in his body, arm yourselves also with the same attitude, because whoever suffers in the body is done with sin.

1 PETER 4:1 NIV

Let us therefore, as many as are perfect, have this attitude; and if in anything you have a different attitude, God will reveal that also to you.

PHILIPPIANS 3:15 NASB

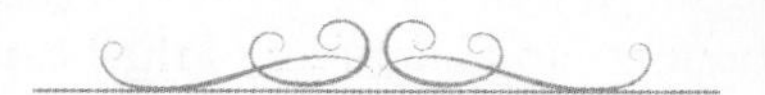

Come, Thou Fount of every blessing,
Tune my heart to sing Thy grace;
Streams of mercy, never ceasing,
Call for songs of loudest praise.

Teach me some melodious sonnet,
Sung by flaming tongues above.
Praise the mount, I'm fixed upon it,
Mount of Thy redeeming love.

"Come, Thou Fount of Every Blessing," Robert Robinson

Busyness

Lord, when my heart is overwhelmed and I can't keep up with it all, please show me how to slow down from my busyness and spend more time with You. I need the rest that comes from being in Your presence. Help me keep things in balance, Father. Amen.

By the seventh day God had finished the work he had been doing; so on the seventh day he rested from all his work.

GENESIS 2:2 NIV

"Come to me, all you who are weary and burdened, and I will give you rest. Take my yoke upon you and learn from me, for I am gentle and humble in heart, and you will find rest for your souls. For my yoke is easy and my burden is light."

MATTHEW 11:28–30 NIV

By the seventh day God had finished the work he had been doing. So on that day he rested from all his work. God blessed the seventh day and made it holy. He blessed it because on that day he rested from all the work he had done.

GENESIS 2:2–3 NIRV

Then, because so many people were coming and going
that [the disciples] did not even have a chance to eat,
[Jesus] said to them, "Come with me by yourselves
to a quiet place and get some rest."

Mark 6:31 NIV

"Remember to keep the Sabbath day holy. Do all your
work in six days. But the seventh day is a sabbath to honor
the Lord your God. Do not do any work on that day.
The same command applies to your sons and daughters,
your male and female servants, and your animals. It also
applies to any outsiders who live in your towns. In six days
the Lord made the heavens, the earth, the sea and everything
in them. But he rested on the seventh day. So the Lord
blessed the Sabbath day and made it holy."

Exodus 20:8–11 NIrV

I said, "Oh, that I had the wings of a dove!
I would fly away and be at rest."

Psalm 55:6 NIV

It is vain for you to rise up early, to retire late, to eat the bread
of painful labors; for He gives to His beloved even in his sleep.

Psalm 127:2 NASB

Then Jesus said to the Pharisees, "The Sabbath day was made to help people; they were not made to be ruled by the Sabbath day."

MARK 2:27 NCV

The LORD is my shepherd; I have everything I need. He lets me rest in green pastures. He leads me to calm water. He gives me new strength. He leads me on paths that are right for the good of his name. Even if I walk through a very dark valley, I will not be afraid, because you are with me. Your rod and your shepherd's staff comfort me.

PSALM 23:1–4 NCV

Be still before the LORD and wait patiently for him;
do not fret when people succeed in their ways,
when they carry out their wicked schemes.

PSALM 37:7 NIV

There remains, then, a Sabbath-rest for the people of God; for anyone who enters God's rest also rests from their works, just as God did from his. Let us, therefore, make every effort to enter that rest, so that no one will perish by following their example of disobedience.

HEBREWS 4:9–11 NIV

I come to the garden alone,
While the dew is still on the roses,
And the voice I hear falling on my ear
The Son of God discloses.

And He walks with me, and He talks with me,
And He tells me I am His own;
And the joy we share as we tarry there,
None other has ever known.

"In the Garden," C. Austin Miles

Church Family

I'm so grateful for the body of Christ, Lord. It's so wonderful to have like-minded people surrounding me, especially when I'm feeling overwhelmed. Thank You for Your Church, Father. Amen.

Now you are the body of Christ,
and each one of you is a part of it.
1 CORINTHIANS 12:27 NIV

He gave all these people so that they might prepare God's people to serve. Then the body of Christ will be built up.
EPHESIANS 4:12 NIRV

Let the peace of Christ rule in your hearts, to which indeed you were called in one body; and be thankful.
COLOSSIANS 3:15 NASB

"And I tell you that you are Peter, and on this rock I will build my church, and the gates of Hades will not overcome it."
MATTHEW 16:18 NIV

So the church throughout all Judea and Galilee and Samaria enjoyed peace, being built up; and going on in the fear of the Lord and in the comfort of the Holy Spirit, it continued to increase.

ACTS 9:31 NASB

So the churches were strengthened in the faith and grew daily in numbers.

ACTS 16:5 NIV

"So guard yourselves and God's people. Feed and shepherd God's flock—his church, purchased with his own blood—over which the Holy Spirit has appointed you as elders."

ACTS 20:28 NLT

I appeal to you, brothers and sisters, in the name of our Lord Jesus Christ, that all of you agree with one another in what you say and that there be no divisions among you, but that you be perfectly united in mind and thought.

1 CORINTHIANS 1:10 NIV

First, God chose some people to be apostles and prophets and teachers for the church. But he also chose some to work miracles or heal the sick or help others or be leaders or speak different kinds of languages.

1 Corinthians 12:28 CEV

And to present her to himself as a radiant church, without stain or wrinkle or any other blemish, but holy and blameless.

Ephesians 5:27 NIV

None of us hate our own bodies. We provide for them and take good care of them, just as Christ does for the church.

Ephesians 5:29 CEV

This is a profound mystery—but I am talking about Christ and the church.

Ephesians 5:32 NIV

Blest be the tie that binds
Our hearts in Christian love;
The fellowship of kindred minds
Is like to that above.

Before our Father's throne,
We pour our ardent prayers;
Our fears, our hopes, our aims are one,
Our comforts and our cares.

We share our mutual woes,
Our mutual burdens bear;
And often for each other flows
The sympathizing tear.

When we asunder part,
It gives us inward pain;
But we shall still be joined in heart,
And hope to meet again.

"Blest Be the Tie That Binds," John Fawcett

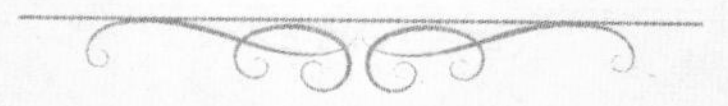

Comforter and Friend

Thank You, God, for sending Your Spirit—my Comforter and Friend. There are days when I feel I can't go on, when I'm too overwhelmed to function, but then Your Spirit whispers, "You can do this," and gives me the courage I need to keep going. I'm so grateful for the Spirit who lives inside of me. Amen.

Now the earth was formless and empty,
darkness was over the surface of the deep,
and the Spirit of God was hovering over the waters.

GENESIS 1:2 NIV

Where can I go to get away from your Spirit?
Where can I run from you?

PSALM 139:7 NCV

Teach me to do your will, for you are my God;
may your good Spirit lead me on level ground.

PSALM 143:10 NIV

"As for me, this is my covenant with them," says the LORD. "My Spirit, who is on you, will not depart from you, and my words that I have put in your mouth will always be on your lips, on the lips of your children and on the lips of their descendants—from this time on and forever," says the LORD.

ISAIAH 59:21 NIV

The Spirit of the LORD will rest on him—the Spirit of wisdom and of understanding, the Spirit of counsel and of might, the Spirit of the knowledge and fear of the LORD.

ISAIAH 11:2 NIV

The Lord GOD has put his Spirit in me, because the LORD has appointed me to tell the good news to the poor. He has sent me to comfort those whose hearts are broken, to tell the captives they are free, and to tell the prisoners they are released.

ISAIAH 61:1 NCV

"And afterward, I will pour out my Spirit on all people. Your sons and daughters will prophesy, your old men will dream dreams, your young men will see visions."

JOEL 2:28 NIV

"Therefore go and make disciples of all nations,
baptizing them in the name of the Father
and of the Son and of the Holy Spirit."

Matthew 28:19 NIV

"I baptize you with water, but he will
baptize you with the Holy Spirit."

Mark 1:8 NIV

Jesus was coming up out of the water. Just then
he saw heaven being torn open. Jesus saw the
Holy Spirit coming down on him like a dove.

Mark 1:10 NIrV

At that same time Jesus was filled with the joy of the Holy
Spirit, and he said, "O Father, Lord of heaven and earth,
thank you for hiding these things from those who think
themselves wise and clever, and for revealing them to the
childlike. Yes, Father, it pleased you to do it this way."

Luke 10:21 NLT

"If you then, though you are evil, know how to give good gifts to your children, how much more will your Father in heaven give the Holy Spirit to those who ask him!"

Luke 11:13 NIV

I tell you for certain that before you can get into God's kingdom, you must be born not only by water, but by the Spirit.

John 3:5 CEV

Spirit of the living God,
Move among us all;
Make us one in heart and mind,
Make us one in love,
Humble, caring,
Selfless, sharing.
Spirit of the living God,
Fill our lives with love.

"Spirit of the Living God," Michael Baughen

Commitment

Sometimes I feel overwhelmed by my commitments, Lord. I take on too much and then regret it after the fact. Please help me do two things: be a person of my word be and a person of balance. I can't do this on my own, Father! I want to be committed, first and foremost, to You. Amen.

Into your hands I commit my spirit;
deliver me, LORD, my faithful God.
PSALM 31:5 NIV

Whatever you do, work heartily,
as for the Lord and not for men.
COLOSSIANS 3:23 ESV

Commit your way to the LORD;
trust in him and he will do this.
PSALM 37:5 NIV

Commit to the LORD whatever you do,
and he will establish your plans.
PROVERBS 16:3 NIV

"Now I am putting you in the care of God and the message about his grace. It is able to give you strength, and it will give you the blessings God has for all his holy people."

ACTS 20:32 NCV

If I preach because I want to, I get a reward.
If I preach because I have to, I'm only doing my duty.

1 CORINTHIANS 9:17 NIRV

Do your best to present yourself to God as one approved, a worker who has no need to be ashamed, rightly handling the word of truth.

2 TIMOTHY 2:15 ESV

So then, those who suffer according to God's will should commit themselves to their faithful Creator and continue to do good.

1 PETER 4:19 NIV

Great is Thy faithfulness,
O God my Father;
There is no shadow of turning with Thee;
Thou changest not,
Thy compassions they fail not;
As Thou hast been, Thou forever wilt be.

Great is Thy faithfulness!
Great is Thy faithfulness!
Morning by morning new mercies I see.
All I have needed Thy hand hath provided;
Great is Thy faithfulness, Lord, unto me!

Summer and winter and springtime and harvest,
Sun, moon, and stars in their courses above,
Join with all nature in manifold witness
To Thy great faithfulness, mercy, and love.

Pardon for sin and a peace that endureth,
Thine own dear presence to cheer and to guide;
Strength for today and bright hope for tomorrow,
Blessings all mine, with ten thousand beside!

"Great Is Thy Faithfulness," Thomas Chisholm

Consequences

Lord, I've faced consequences time and time again in my life. Some are good, others, not so much. Still, I'm on a learning curve, and for that, I'm very grateful. . .even if I often feel overwhelmed in the moment. I know I can trust You, Father. Keep teaching me. I am a willing learner. Amen.

Do not be deceived: God is not mocked,
for whatever one sows, that will he also reap.
GALATIANS 6:7 ESV

"From now on the Israelites must not go near the tent of meeting, or they will bear the consequences of their sin and will die."
NUMBERS 18:22 NIV

The rod and reproof give wisdom, but a child left to himself brings shame to his mother.
PROVERBS 29:15 ESV

"Therefore this is what the Sovereign LORD says: Since you have forgotten me and turned your back on me, you must bear the consequences of your lewdness and prostitution."
EZEKIEL 23:35 NIV

Train up a child in the way he should go;
even when he is old he will not depart from it.
PROVERBS 22:6 ESV

For the wages of sin is death, but the free gift of God is eternal life in Christ Jesus our Lord.
ROMANS 6:23 ESV

"And if you faithfully obey the voice of the LORD your God, being careful to do all his commandments that I command you today, the LORD your God will set you high above all the nations of the earth. And all these blessings shall come upon you and overtake you, if you obey the voice of the LORD your God. Blessed shall you be in the city, and blessed shall you be in the field. Blessed shall be the fruit of your womb and the fruit of your ground and the fruit of your cattle, the increase of your herds and the young of your flock. Blessed shall be your basket and your kneading bowl. Blessed shall you be when you come in, and blessed shall you be when you go out."
DEUTERONOMY 28:1–6 ESV

I'll live for my Savior wherever I go,
And more and more strive His sweet spirit to show;
His love and His grace will not fail me, I know,
I'll live for Him day by day.

I'll live for Him day by day,
I'll live for Him day by day,
My Savior and Guide,
For me crucified,
I'll live for Him day by day.

"I'll Live for My Savior Wherever I Go," Gertrude Everett

Contentment

I can be content in You, Lord, even when things around me are spinning out of control. I'm still learning how to do that, of course, but I'm making progress. Whether I'm feeling overwhelmed or at peace, You are teaching me to be content in whatever state I'm in. Thank You for that! Amen.

But godliness with contentment is great gain.

1 Timothy 6:6 NIV

Those who respect the Lord will live
and be satisfied, unbothered by trouble.

Proverbs 19:23 NCV

But if we have food and clothing,
we will be content with that.

1 Timothy 6:8 NIV

A man will be satisfied with good by the fruit of his words,
and the deeds of a man's hands will return to him.

Proverbs 12:14 NASB

I have made myself calm and content like a young child in its mother's arms. Deep down inside me, I am as content as a young child.

PSALM 131:2 NIRV

As for me, I shall behold Your face in righteousness; I will be satisfied with Your likeness when I awake.

PSALM 17:15 NASB

I know what it is to be in need, and I know what it is to have plenty. I have learned the secret of being content in any and every situation, whether well fed or hungry, whether living in plenty or in want.

PHILIPPIANS 4:12 NIV

They all ate and were satisfied, and the disciples picked up twelve basketfuls of broken pieces that were left over.

MATTHEW 14:20 NIV

Blessed are you who are hungry now. You will be satisfied. Blessed are you who are sad now. You will laugh.

LUKE 6:21 NIRV

When peace like a river attendeth my way,
When sorrows like sea billows roll;
Whatever my lot, Thou hast taught me to say,
It is well, it is well with my soul.

Though Satan should buffet, though trials should come,
Let this blest assurance control:
That Christ has regarded my helpless estate,
And has shed His own blood for my soul.

My sin—oh, the bliss of this glorious thought!—
My sin, not in part, but the whole,
Is nailed to the cross and I bear it no more;
Praise the Lord, praise the Lord, O my soul!

And, Lord, haste the day when my faith shall be sight,
The clouds be rolled back as a scroll;
The trump shall resound and the Lord shall descend;
Even so, it is well with my soul.

"It Is Well with My Soul," Horatio Spafford

Courage

I don't always have the courage I need, Lord. Of course, I'm usually depending on myself, not You. Today I ask that You give me courage to overcome the obstacles in my life. I give You my fears. Please replace them with godly bravery! Amen.

When they saw the courage of Peter and John and realized that they were unschooled, ordinary men, they were astonished and they took note that these men had been with Jesus.

ACTS 4:13 NIV

The following night the Lord stood near Paul and said, "Take courage! As you have testified about me in Jerusalem, so you must also testify in Rome."

ACTS 23:11 NIV

"So men, have courage. I trust in God that everything will happen as his angel told me."

ACTS 27:25 NCV

"Be strong and courageous. Do not be afraid or terrified because of them, for the LORD your God goes with you; he will never leave you nor forsake you."

DEUTERONOMY 31:6 NIV

Be on your guard. Remain strong in the faith. Be brave.

1 CORINTHIANS 16:13 NIRV

"Have I not commanded you? Be strong and courageous. Do not be afraid; do not be discouraged, for the LORD your God will be with you wherever you go."

JOSHUA 1:9 NIV

Praise to the Lord, the Almighty, the King of creation!
O my soul, praise Him, for He is thy health and salvation!
All ye who hear, now to His temple draw near;
Praise Him in glad adoration!

"PRAISE TO THE LORD, THE ALMIGHTY," JOACHIM NEANDER

Decisions

I must confess, Lord, some of my stresses come from my own poor choices and decisions. I know I can't go backwards, but with Your help I can make better decisions from this point on—ones that will bring me peace, not turmoil. Help me, I pray. Amen.

"So, Job, should God reward you as you want when you refuse to change? You must decide, not I, so tell me what you know."

JOB 34:33 NCV

The believers decided to provide help for the brothers and sisters living in Judea. All of them helped as much as they could.

ACTS 11:29 NIRV

Blessed are those whose strength comes from you.
They have firmly decided to travel to your temple.

PSALM 84:5 NIRV

"Why can't you decide for yourselves what is right?"

LUKE 12:57 NCV

So let's stop condemning each other. Decide instead to live in such a way that you will not cause another believer to stumble and fall.

ROMANS 14:13 NLT

"But when I found that he had committed nothing deserving of death, and that he himself had appealed to Augustus, I decided to send him."

ACTS 25:25 NKJV

"What you decide to do will be done. Light will shine on the path you take."

JOB 22:28 NIRV

For I decided that while I was with you I would forget everything except Jesus Christ, the one who was crucified.

1 CORINTHIANS 2:2 NLT

All the way my Savior leads me;
What have I to ask beside?
Can I doubt His tender mercy,
Who through life has been my Guide?
Heav'nly peace, divinest comfort,
Here by faith in Him to dwell!
For I know, whate'er befall me,
Jesus doeth all things well;
For I know, whate'er befall me,
Jesus doeth all things well.

"All the Way My Savior Leads Me," Fanny Crosby

Depression

So many people around me are struggling, Lord. I feel the weight of their pain so deeply at times. I've gone through low seasons, too. Today I choose to turn my eyes to You, to lift my head and my heart. Thank You for being there when I call, Father. I need You every day. Amen.

The LORD hears his people when they call to him for help. He rescues them from all their troubles. The LORD is close to the brokenhearted; he rescues those whose spirits are crushed.

PSALM 34:17–18 NLT

"Come to me, all who labor and are heavy laden, and I will give you rest."

MATTHEW 11:28 ESV

Fear not, for I am with you; be not dismayed, for I am your God; I will strengthen you, I will help you, I will uphold you with my righteous right hand.

ISAIAH 41:10 ESV

Answer me quickly, O LORD, my spirit fails; do not hide Your face from me, or I will become like those who go down to the pit. Let me hear Your lovingkindness in the morning; for I trust in You; teach me the way in which I should walk; for to You I lift up my soul.

PSALM 143:7–8 NASB

The LORD is near to the brokenhearted
and saves the crushed in spirit.

PSALM 34:18 ESV

But you, LORD, are a shield around me, my glory,
the One who lifts my head high.

PSALM 3:3 NIV

A glad heart makes a happy face;
a broken heart crushes the spirit.

PROVERBS 15:13 NLT

Arise, shine, for your light has come, and the glory of the LORD has risen upon you.

ISAIAH 60:1 ESV

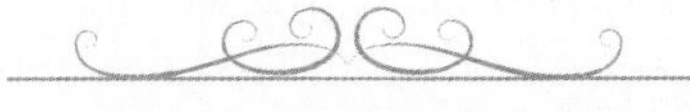

There is a balm in Gilead
To make the wounded whole,
There is a balm in Gilead
To heal the sin-sick soul.

Sometimes I feel discouraged
And think my work's in vain,
But then the Holy Spirit
Revives my soul again.

"THERE IS A BALM IN GILEAD," SPIRITUAL (AUTHOR UNKNOWN)

Discipline

Discipline. Most of us aren't a fan of this word, Father. I mean, we want to be disciplined, in general, but when it comes to living it out daily, not so much. Help me, Father, as I strive to become more disciplined—in my prayer life, my health, and my relationships. Amen.

Know then in your heart that as a man disciplines his son, so the LORD your God disciplines you.

DEUTERONOMY 8:5 NIV

My child, do not reject the LORD's discipline, and don't get angry when he corrects you.

PROVERBS 3:11 NCV

The LORD disciplines those he loves, as a father the son he delights in.

PROVERBS 3:12 NIV

He is on the path of life who heeds instruction, but he who ignores reproof goes astray.

PROVERBS 10:17 NASB

A fool spurns a parent's discipline,
but whoever heeds correction shows prudence.

Proverbs 15:5 NIV

Discipline your children, and they will give you
peace of mind and will make your heart glad.

Proverbs 29:17 NLT

Nevertheless, when we are judged in this way by
the Lord, we are being disciplined so that we will
not be finally condemned with the world.

1 Corinthians 11:32 NIV

For God has not given us a spirit of fear and timidity,
but of power, love, and self-discipline.

2 Timothy 1:7 NLT

Rather, he must be hospitable, one who loves what is good, who is self-controlled, upright, holy and disciplined.

TITUS 1:8 NIV

And have you forgotten the encouraging words God spoke to you as his children? He said, "My child, don't make light of the LORD's discipline, and don't give up when he corrects you."

HEBREWS 12:5 NLT

Endure hardship as discipline; God is treating you as his children. For what children are not disciplined by their father?

HEBREWS 12:7 NIV

We do not enjoy being disciplined. It is painful at the time, but later, after we have learned from it, we have peace, because we start living in the right way.

HEBREWS 12:11 NCV

Savior! teach me, day by day,
Love's sweet lesson to obey;
Sweeter lesson cannot be,
Loving Him who first loved me.

With a childlike heart of love,
At Thy bidding may I move;
Prompt to serve and follow Thee,
Loving Him who first loved me.

Teach me all Thy steps to trace,
Strong to follow in Thy grace;
Learning how to love from Thee,
Loving Him who first loved me.

"SAVIOR, TEACH ME, DAY BY DAY," JANE E. LEESON

Faith

Lord, when my heart is overwhelmed, it's usually because I've taken my eyes off of You. Increase my faith, Father! Remind me that keeping my trust in You is the only way to overcome. Amen.

Faith means being sure of the things we hope for and knowing that something is real even if we do not see it. Faith is the reason we remember great people who lived in the past. It is by faith we understand that the whole world was made by God's command so what we see was made by something that cannot be seen.

HEBREWS 11:1–3 NCV

Some men brought to him a paralyzed man, lying on a mat. When Jesus saw their faith, he said to the man, "Take heart, son; your sins are forgiven."

MATTHEW 9:2 NIV

Jesus turned and saw her. "Dear woman, don't give up hope," he said. "Your faith has healed you." The woman was healed at that very moment.

MATTHEW 9:22 NIRV

Then he touched their eyes and said,
"According to your faith let it be done to you."
Matthew 9:29 NIV

And He said to them, "Because of the littleness of your faith; for truly I say to you, if you have faith the size of a mustard seed, you will say to this mountain, 'Move from here to there,' and it will move; and nothing will be impossible to you."
Matthew 17:20 NASB

"Have faith in God," Jesus answered.
Mark 11:22 NIV

"I tell you, God will see that things are made right for them. He will make sure it happens quickly. But when the Son of Man comes, will he find people on earth who have faith?"
Luke 18:8 NIrV

"By faith in the name of Jesus, this man whom you see and know was made strong. It is Jesus' name and the faith that comes through him that has completely healed him, as you can all see."

ACTS 3:16 NIV

Through him we received grace and apostleship to call all the Gentiles to the obedience that comes from faith for his name's sake.

ROMANS 1:5 NIV

First, I thank my God through Jesus Christ for you all, because your faith is being proclaimed throughout the whole world.

ROMANS 1:8 NASB

Therefore, the promise comes by faith, so that it may be by grace and may be guaranteed to all Abraham's offspring—not only to those who are of the law but also to those who have the faith of Abraham. He is the father of us all.

ROMANS 4:16 NIV

My faith looks up to Thee,
Thou Lamb of Calvary, Savior divine!
Now hear me while I pray; take all my guilt away;
O let me from this day be wholly Thine!

"My Faith Looks Up to Thee," Ray Palmer

Family Matters

Father, when I'm feeling overwhelmed, I think of my family and am instantly comforted. Thank You for surrounding me with people who care for me and support me. I'm so grateful for every single person You've placed in my life (even the difficult ones). Amen.

But he rescues the poor from trouble and
increases their families like flocks of sheep.

Psalm 107:41 NLT

Your wife shall be like a fruitful vine within your house,
your children like olive plants around your table.

Psalm 128:3 NASB

Both the one who makes people holy and those who
are made holy are of the same family. So Jesus is
not ashamed to call them brothers and sisters.

Hebrews 2:11 NIV

As all the men of Judah stood before the LORD
with their little ones, wives, and children.
2 Chronicles 20:13 NLT

She gets up while it is still night; she provides food
for her family and portions for her female servants.
Proverbs 31:15 NIV

To the woman he said, "I will make your pains in childbearing
very severe; with painful labor you will give birth to children.
Your desire will be for your husband, and he will rule over you."
Genesis 3:16 NIV

They replied, "Believe in the Lord Jesus,
and you will be saved—you and your household."
Acts 16:31 NIV

He must manage his own family well,
having children who respect and obey him.

1 Timothy 3:4 NLT

"Now then, please swear to me by the Lord that you
will show kindness to my family, because I have
shown kindness to you. Give me a sure sign."

Joshua 2:12 NIV

Therefore, as we have opportunity, let us do good to all people,
especially to those who belong to the family of believers.

Galatians 6:10 NIV

But if a widow has children or grandchildren, these should
learn first of all to put their religion into practice by caring
for their own family and so repaying their parents and
grandparents, for this is pleasing to God.

1 Timothy 5:4 NIV

Come, ye thankful people, come,
Raise the song of harvest home;
All is safely gathered in,
Ere the winter storms begin.
God our Maker doth provide
For our wants to be supplied;
Come to God's own temple, come,
Raise the song of harvest home.

"COME, YE THANKFUL PEOPLE, COME," HENRY ALFORD

Forever and Ever

Father, so many times I walk through seasons that feel like they just won't quit. I'm overwhelmed, exhausted, and ready to give up. During these times it's more important than ever to have a "forever" perspective. Please help me with that, Lord. I have to see beyond today. I need Your eternal perspective. Give me Your eyes to see so that my overwhelmed heart can quiet itself. Amen.

He has made everything beautiful in its time. He has also set eternity in the human heart; yet no one can fathom what God has done from beginning to end.

ECCLESIASTES 3:11 NIV

Give thanks to the LORD because he is good.
His love continues forever.

PSALM 136:1 NCV

The fear of the LORD is clean, enduring forever; the judgments of the LORD are true; they are righteous altogether.

PSALM 19:9 NASB

Surely your goodness and love will follow me all the days of my life, and I will dwell in the house of the LORD forever.

PSALM 23:6 NIV

Jesus Christ is the same yesterday and today and forever.

HEBREWS 13:8 NLV

Everyone who competes in the games goes into strict training. They do it to get a crown that will not last, but we do it to get a crown that will last forever.

1 CORINTHIANS 9:25 NIV

The LORD sits enthroned over the flood;
the LORD is enthroned as King forever.

PSALM 29:10 NIV

But the plans of the LORD stand firm forever,
the purposes of his heart through all generations.

PSALM 33:11 NIV

As for me, You hold me up in my honesty.
And You set me beside You forever.

Psalm 41:12 NLV

My flesh and my heart may fail, but God is the strength of my heart and my portion forever.

Psalm 73:26 NIV

I will declare that your love stands firm forever, that you have established your faithfulness in heaven itself.

Psalm 89:2 NIV

He has sent redemption to His people; He has ordained His covenant forever; holy and awesome is His name.

Psalm 111:9 NASB

The righteous will inherit the land and dwell in it forever.

Psalm 37:29 niv

"I am the living bread that came down from heaven. Whoever eats this bread will live forever. This bread is my flesh, which I will give for the life of the world."

John 6:51 niv

"I will ask the Father. And he will give you another friend to help you and to be with you forever."

John 14:16 nirv

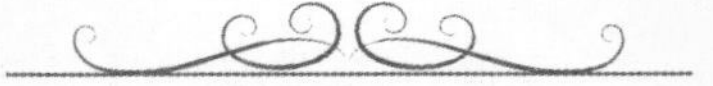

Jesus, my Savior, look on me,
For I am weary and oppressed;
I come to cast myself on Thee:
Thou art my Rest.

Look down on me, for I am weak;
I feel the toilsome journey's length;
Thine aid omnipotent I seek:
Thou art my Strength.

I am bewildered on my way,
Dark and tempestuous is the night;
O send Thou forth some cheering ray:
Thou art my Light.

"JESUS, MY SAVIOR, LOOK ON ME," CHARLOTTE ELLIOT

Foundation

Father, I'm learning (sometimes the hard way) about building a firm foundation on You. When I strike out on my own without a solid foundation, my proverbial building comes crumbling down, and I end up overwhelmed and frustrated. Keep me focused on You, the Master Builder, I pray. Amen.

When the earth quakes and its people live in turmoil,
I am the one who keeps its foundations firm.

PSALM 75:3 NLT

Fear of the LORD is the foundation of true knowledge,
but fools despise wisdom and discipline.

PROVERBS 1:7 NLT

"But the one who has heard and has not acted accordingly, is like a man who built a house on the ground without any foundation; and the torrent burst against it and immediately it collapsed, and the ruin of that house was great."

LUKE 6:49 NASB

By the grace God has given me, I laid a foundation as
a wise builder, and someone else is building on it.
But each one should build with care.

1 CORINTHIANS 3:10 NIV

Therefore leaving the elementary teaching about the Christ,
let us press on to maturity, not laying again a foundation
of repentance from dead works and of faith toward God.

HEBREWS 6:1 NASB

He set the earth on its foundations;
it can never be moved.

PSALM 104:5 NIV

"The rain came down, the streams rose, and the winds
blew and beat against that house; yet it did not fall,
because it had its foundation on the rock."

MATTHEW 7:25 NIV

How firm a foundation, ye saints of the Lord,
Is laid for your faith in His excellent Word!
What more can He say than to you He hath said,
You, who unto the Savior for refuge have fled?

"How Firm a Foundation," Author Unknown

Frustration

How easily I'm frustrated, Lord! I know it's because I take on too much without asking for Your advice first. Today I'm asking You to help me with these feelings of frustration, Father. Ease them, I pray. Calm my heart and give me peace. Amen.

Do not fret because of those who are evil
or be envious of those who do wrong.

PSALM 37:1 NIV

For God alone, O my soul, wait in silence, for my hope is from him. He only is my rock and my salvation, my fortress; I shall not be shaken. On God rests my salvation and my glory; my mighty rock, my refuge is God. Trust in him at all times, O people; pour out your heart before him; God is a refuge for us.

PSALM 62:5–8 ESV

Be still before the LORD and wait patiently for him;
do not fret when people succeed in their ways,
when they carry out their wicked schemes.

PSALM 37:7 NIV

Refrain from anger and turn from wrath;
do not fret—it leads only to evil.
PSALM 37:8 NIV

Do not fret because of evildoers
or be envious of the wicked.
PROVERBS 24:19 NIV

And let us not grow weary of doing good, for in
due season we will reap, if we do not give up.
GALATIANS 6:9 ESV

What a Friend we have in Jesus, all our sins and griefs to bear!
What a privilege to carry everything to God in prayer!
O what peace we often forfeit, O what needless pain we bear,
all because we do not carry everything to God in prayer.

"What a Friend We Have in Jesus," Joseph M. Scriven

Gentleness

Lord, I want to have a gentle spirit, one that guides my every word and laces my comments with grace, not bitterness. Please pour out Your gentleness on me, Father, so that I can be an example to others. Amen.

Let your gentleness be evident to all.
The Lord is near.
PHILIPPIANS 4:5 NIV

But you, O man of God, flee these things and pursue righteousness, godliness, faith, love, patience, gentleness.
1 TIMOTHY 6:11 NKJV

"Take my yoke upon you and learn from me, for I am gentle and humble in heart, and you will find rest for your souls."
MATTHEW 11:29 NIV

Always be humble, gentle, and patient,
accepting each other in love.
EPHESIANS 4:2 NCV

No, your beauty should come from within you—
the beauty of a gentle and quiet spirit that will
never be destroyed and is very precious to God.

1 PETER 3:4 NCV

You are God's chosen people. You are holy and dearly loved.
So put on tender mercy and kindness as if they were
your clothes. Don't be proud. Be gentle and patient.

COLOSSIANS 3:12 NIRV

Gentle Jesus, meek and mild,
Look upon a little child;
Pity my simplicity,
Suffer me to come to Thee.

Loving Jesus, gentle Lamb,
In Thy gracious hands I am;
Make me, Savior, what Thou art,
Live Thyself within my heart.

"GENTLE JESUS, MEEK AND MILD," CHARLES WESLEY

Goal Setting/Planning

Sometimes I forget to count the cost before I make my plans, Lord. I dive in, ready to conquer new tasks, and get overwhelmed because I didn't strategize. The next time I get ready to conquer something new, help me make a solid plan first. May my goals and plans always be committed to You, Father! Amen.

"But you, take courage! Do not let your hands be weak, for your work shall be rewarded."

2 Chronicles 15:7 ESV

Instead, you must worship Christ as Lord of your life. And if someone asks about your hope as a believer, always be ready to explain it.

1 Peter 3:15 NLT

But the noble man devises noble plans; and by noble plans he stands.

Isaiah 32:8 NASB

"For which of you, desiring to build a tower,
does not first sit down and count the cost,
whether he has enough to complete it?"

LUKE 14:28 ESV

The plans of the diligent lead surely to abundance,
but everyone who is hasty comes only to poverty.

PROVERBS 21:5 ESV

"For I know the plans I have for you," says the LORD.
"They are plans for good and not for disaster,
to give you a future and a hope."

JEREMIAH 29:11 NLT

Commit your works to the LORD and
your plans will be established.

PROVERBS 16:3 NASB

Be thou my vision, O Lord of my heart;
Naught be all else to me, save that Thou art;
Thou my best thought, by day or by night,
Waking or sleeping, Thy presence my light.

Be Thou my wisdom, and Thou my true Word;
I ever with Thee and Thou with me, Lord;
Thou my great Father, I Thy true son;
Thou in me dwelling, and I with Thee one.

Riches I heed not, nor man's empty praise;
Thou, mine inheritance, now and always;
Thou and Thou only, first in my heart,
High King of Heaven, my treasure Thou art.

High King of Heaven, my victory won,
May I reach heaven's joys, O bright heaven's Sun!
Heart of my own heart, whatever befall,
Still be my vision, O Ruler of all.

"Be Thou My Vision," Dallan Forgaill

God, Our Father

What a wonderful Father You are, Lord! Like a great Daddy, You wipe away my tears, give me guidance, and hold me close to Your heart. During those seasons when I'm overwhelmed, I'm especially grateful for Your fatherly comfort. Thank You for being there for me, Abba. Amen.

But you are our Father, though Abraham does not know us or Israel acknowledge us; you, LORD, are our Father, our Redeemer from of old is your name.
ISAIAH 63:16 NIV

But LORD, you are our father. We are like clay, and you are the potter; your hands made us all.
ISAIAH 64:8 NCV

Do we not all have one Father? Did not one God create us? Why do we profane the covenant of our ancestors by being unfaithful to one another?
MALACHI 2:10 NIV

"So when you pray, you should pray like this: 'Our Father in heaven, may your name always be kept holy.'"

MATTHEW 6:9 NCV

Because you are his sons, God sent the Spirit of his Son into our hearts, the Spirit who calls out, "*Abba*, Father."

GALATIANS 4:6 NIV

Jesus replied, "Anyone who loves me will obey my teaching. My Father will love them, and we will come to them and make our home with them."

JOHN 14:23 NIV

So that with one accord you may with one voice glorify the God and Father of our Lord Jesus Christ.

ROMANS 15:6 NASB

Give praise to the God and Father of our Lord Jesus Christ!
He is the Father who gives tender love.
All comfort comes from him.

2 CORINTHIANS 1:3 NIRV

I keep asking that the God of our Lord Jesus Christ, the glorious Father, may give you the Spirit of wisdom and revelation, so that you may know him better.

EPHESIANS 1:17 NIV

Praise be to the God and Father of our Lord Jesus Christ! In his great mercy he has given us new birth into a living hope through the resurrection of Jesus Christ from the dead.

1 PETER 1:3 NIV

Father, lead me, for I need Thee
Ev'ry step of life's long way;
Thou alone art e'er unchanging,
Give Thy presence day by day.

Father, lead me now and ever,
For I know Thy way is best,
Fold me closer, fold me closer,
Let me find in Thee sweet rest.

"Father, Lead Me," Author Unknown

God, Our Rock

I love the image of You as a Rock, Lord! Rocks are solid, unmoving. They're firm. Thank You for being a place of safety that I can run to. No shifting sands with You, Lord! Thanks for being my Rock. Amen.

"My God is my rock, in whom I take refuge, my shield and the horn of my salvation. He is my stronghold, my refuge and my savior—from violent people you save me."

2 Samuel 22:3 NIV

"Who is God except the Lord?
Who is the Rock except our God?"

2 Samuel 22:32 NIrV

Praise be to the Lord my Rock, who trains my hands for war, my fingers for battle.

Psalm 144:1 NIV

"The LORD lives! Blessed be my Rock!
Let God be exalted, the Rock of my salvation!"
2 SAMUEL 22:47 NKJV

Since you are my rock and my fortress,
for the sake of your name lead and guide me.
PSALM 31:3 NIV

From a place far away I call out to you. I call out as my heart gets weaker. Lead me to the safety of a rock that is high above me.
PSALM 61:2 NIRV

But the LORD has become my fortress,
and my God the rock in whom I take refuge.
PSALM 94:22 NIV

He only is my rock and my salvation;
He is my defense; I shall not be moved.
PSALM 62:6 NKJV

Be my rock of refuge, to which I can always go; give the command to save me, for you are my rock and my fortress.

Psalm 71:3 NIV

Come, let us sing with joy to the Lord.
Let us give a loud shout to the Rock who saves us.

Psalm 95:1 NIrV

"And I tell you that you are Peter, and on this rock I will build my church, and the gates of Hades will not overcome it."

Matthew 16:18 NIV

"They are like a man building a house, who dug down deep and laid the foundation on rock. When a flood came, the torrent struck that house but could not shake it, because it was well built."

Luke 6:48 NIV

My hope is built on nothing less
Than Jesus' blood and righteousness;
I dare not trust the sweetest frame,
But wholly lean on Jesus' name.

On Christ, the solid Rock, I stand;
All other ground is sinking sand;
All other ground is sinking sand.

"My Hope Is Built on Nothing Less," Edward Mote

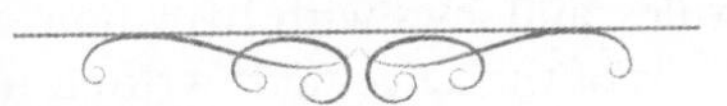

God's Presence

When I'm weary, spending time in Your presence is the very best form of therapy, Lord. There in that secret place, under the shadow of Your wing, I find safety, peace, and rest. Ah! Just what the doctor ordered. Thank You, Father, for wooing me into that holy place. Amen.

The LORD replied, "My Presence will go with you, and I will give you rest."
EXODUS 33:14 NIV

The king stood by the pillar and made an agreement in the presence of the LORD to follow the LORD and obey his commands, rules, and laws with his whole being, and to obey the words of the agreement written in this book. Then all the people promised to obey the agreement.
2 KINGS 23:3 NCV

Then I was constantly at his side. I was filled with delight day after day, rejoicing always in his presence.
PROVERBS 8:30 NIV

Enter into the rock, and hide in the dust,
from the terror of the LORD and the glory of His majesty.

ISAIAH 2:10 NKJV

"In my vision at night I looked, and there before me was one like a son of man, coming with the clouds of heaven. He approached the Ancient of Days and was led into his presence."

DANIEL 7:13 NIV

The mountains quake before him and the hills melt away. The earth trembles at his presence, the world and all who live in it.

NAHUM 1:5 NIV

This is how we know we are Christians. It will give
our heart comfort for sure when we stand before Him.

1 JOHN 3:19 NLV

To him who is able to keep you from stumbling and to present you before his glorious presence without fault and with great joy—to the only God our Savior be glory, majesty, power and authority, through Jesus Christ our Lord, before all ages, now and forevermore! Amen.

JUDE 1:24–25 NIV

The LORD is in his holy temple; the LORD is on his heavenly throne. He observes everyone on earth; his eyes examine them.

PSALM 11:4 NIV

"But the LORD is in His holy temple.
Let all the earth keep silence before Him."

HABAKKUK 2:20 NKJV

Jesus! I am resting, resting
In the joy of what Thou art;
I am finding out the greatness
Of Thy loving heart.

Thou hast bid me gaze upon Thee,
And Thy beauty fills my soul,
For, by Thy transforming power,
Thou hast made me whole.

Jesus! I am resting, resting
In the joy of what Thou art;
I am finding out the greatness
Of Thy loving heart.

"Jesus, I Am Resting, Resting," Jean S. Pigott

God's Word

Your Word is precious to me, Lord! It amazes me that Your precepts are written down so that I can study and learn them. Now, to make the time to do so! Staying in the Word is my best chance for success, Father. Help me to spend more time with You. Amen.

All Scripture is God-breathed and is useful for teaching, rebuking, correcting and training in righteousness.
2 TIMOTHY 3:16 NIV

Turn my eyes away from worthless things;
preserve my life according to your word.
PSALM 119:37 NIV

Your eternal word, O LORD, stands firm in heaven.
PSALM 119:89 NLT

Then he opened their minds so they
could understand the Scriptures.

LUKE 24:45 NIV

Such things were written in the Scriptures long ago to teach us. And the Scriptures give us hope and encouragement as we wait patiently for God's promises to be fulfilled.

ROMANS 15:4 NLT

For in Scripture it says: "See, I lay a stone in Zion, a chosen and precious cornerstone, and the one who trusts in him will never be put to shame."

1 PETER 2:6 NIV

For I handed on to you as of first importance what I in turn had received: that Christ died for our sins in accordance with the scriptures.

1 CORINTHIANS 15:3 NRSV

Until I come, devote yourself to the public reading of Scripture, to preaching and to teaching.

1 TIMOTHY 4:13 NIV

Holy Bible, book divine,
Precious treasure, thou art mine;
Mine to tell me whence I came;
Mine to teach me what I am.

"HOLY BIBLE, BOOK DIVINE," JOHN BURTON

Goodness

Your unspeakable goodness propels me, Lord! I want to be like You, pouring out goodness on others as You've poured it out on me. Give me special opportunities, I pray, that I might surprise people with Your goodness. May Your heart be shown in all I do and say. Amen.

But you, Sovereign Lord, help me for your name's sake;
out of the goodness of your love, deliver me.
Psalm 109:21 NIV

They shall eagerly utter the memory of Your abundant goodness and will shout joyfully of Your righteousness.
Psalm 145:7 NASB

For it is impossible to bring back to repentance those who were once enlightened—those who have experienced the good things of heaven and shared in the Holy Spirit, who have tasted the goodness of the word of God and the power of the age to come—and who then turn away from God. It is impossible to bring such people back to repentance; by rejecting the Son of God, they themselves are nailing him to the cross once again and holding him up to public shame.
Hebrews 6:4–7 NLT

Therefore we also pray always for you that our God would count you worthy of this calling, and fulfill all the good pleasure of His goodness and the work of faith with power.
2 Thessalonians 1:11 NKJV

His divine power has given us everything we need for a godly life through our knowledge of him who called us by his own glory and goodness.
2 Peter 1:3 NIV

In view of all this, make every effort to respond to God's promises. Supplement your faith with a generous provision of moral excellence, and moral excellence with knowledge.
2 Peter 1:5 NLT

Blessed assurance, Jesus is mine!
Oh, what a foretaste of glory divine!
Heir of salvation, purchase of God,
Born of His Spirit, washed in His blood.

This is my story, this is my song,
Praising my Savior all the day long;
This is my story, this is my song,
Praising my Savior all the day long.

Perfect submission, perfect delight,
Visions of rapture now burst on my sight:
Angels descending bring from above
Echoes of mercy, whispers of love.

Perfect submission, all is at rest,
I in my Savior am happy and blest;
Watching and waiting, looking above,
Filled with His goodness, lost in His love.

"BLESSED ASSURANCE," FANNY CROSBY

Gossip

What a challenge, Lord, not to gossip! I try so hard not to talk about others behind their backs, but then I slip up. Oops. I'm grateful for Your forgiveness. I know that gossip doesn't just hurt the one I'm talking about, Father—it also hurts me because it makes me focus on the negative, not the positive. Help me make better choices, I pray. Amen.

A perverse person stirs up conflict,
and a gossip separates close friends.
PROVERBS 16:28 NIV

Let no corrupting talk come out of your mouths,
but only such as is good for building up, as fits the
occasion, that it may give grace to those who hear.
EPHESIANS 4:29 ESV

Have nothing to do with godless myths and old
wives' tales; rather, train yourself to be godly.
1 TIMOTHY 4:7 NIV

A dishonest man spreads strife,
and a whisperer separates close friends.
PROVERBS 16:28 ESV

Without wood a fire goes out;
without a gossip a quarrel dies down.

Proverbs 26:20 NIV

"Let everyone be on guard against his neighbor,
and do not trust any brother; because every brother deals
craftily, and every neighbor goes about as a slanderer."

Jeremiah 9:4 NASB

Whoever goes about slandering reveals secrets;
therefore do not associate with a simple babbler.

Proverbs 20:19 ESV

If anyone thinks he is religious and does not bridle his tongue
but deceives his heart, this person's religion is worthless.

James 1:26 ESV

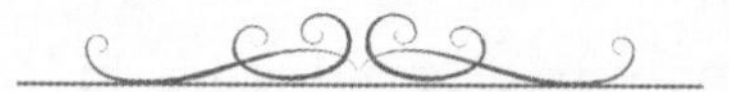

Let the words of my mouth,
Let the words of my mouth
And the meditations of my heart
Be acceptable in Thy sight;
Wilt Thou teach me how to serve Thee,
Wilt Thou teach me how to pray?

"Let the Words of My Mouth," Author Unknown

Grace

Lord, I'm amazed by Your grace, Your riches at Your Son's expense. Because of His gift on Calvary, my heart, soul, and spirit are set free. I can rest easy in the assurance that Your great love has covered it all. For that, I'm eternally thankful.

The Word became flesh and made his dwelling among us. We have seen his glory, the glory of the one and only Son, who came from the Father, full of grace and truth.

John 1:14 NIV

And with great power the apostles were giving testimony to the resurrection of the Lord Jesus, and abundant grace was upon them all.

Acts 4:33 NASB

But my life means nothing to me. My only goal is to finish the race. I want to complete the work the Lord Jesus has given me. He wants me to tell others about the good news of God's grace.

Acts 20:24 NIrV

Through him we received grace and apostleship
to call all the Gentiles to the obedience that
comes from faith for his name's sake.

Romans 1:5 NIV

For sin shall not be master over you,
for you are not under law but under grace.

Romans 6:14 NASB

I always thank my God for you. I thank him because of the
grace he has given to you who belong to Christ Jesus.

1 Corinthians 1:4 NIrV

But he said to me, "My grace is sufficient for you,
for my power is made perfect in weakness." Therefore
I will boast all the more gladly about my weaknesses,
so that Christ's power may rest on me.

2 Corinthians 12:9 NIV

For it is by grace you have been saved, through faith—
and this is not from yourselves, it is the gift of God.
EPHESIANS 2:8 NIV

Let your speech always be with grace, seasoned with salt,
that you may know how you ought to answer each one.
COLOSSIANS 4:6 NKJV

For the grace of God has appeared that
offers salvation to all people.
TITUS 2:11 NIV

Amazing grace, how sweet the sound
That saved a wretch like me!
I once was lost but now am found,
Was blind but now I see.

'Twas grace that taught my heart to fear,
And grace my fears relieved;
How precious did that grace appear
The hour I first believed!

The Lord has promised good to me,
His word my hope secures;
He will my shield and portion be
As long as life endures.

Through many dangers, toils, and snares
I have already come;
'Tis grace hath brought me safe thus far,
And grace will lead me home.

When we've been there ten thousand years,
Bright shining as the sun,
We've no less days to sing God's praise
Than when we'd first begun.

"Amazing Grace," John Newton

Gratitude

How can I ever express my gratitude to You, Lord? Not only do You give me rest when I'm weary, peace when I'm anxious, joy when I'm sad, but You also give me eternal life through Your Son, Jesus. There are no words to express my gratitude, Father! Amen.

Let the word of Christ dwell in you richly; teach and admonish one another in all wisdom; and with gratitude in your hearts sing psalms, hymns, and spiritual songs to God.

COLOSSIANS 3:16 NRSV

Sing to the LORD with grateful praise;
make music to our God on the harp.

PSALM 147:7 NIV

I am grateful to Christ Jesus our Lord,
who has strengthened me, because he judged
me faithful and appointed me to his service.

1 TIMOTHY 1:12 NRSV

"But I, with shouts of grateful praise, will sacrifice to you. What I have vowed I will make good. I will say, 'Salvation comes from the LORD.'"

JONAH 2:9 NIV

They risked their lives for me. Not only I but all the churches of the Gentiles are grateful to them.

ROMANS 16:4 NIV

For everything created by God is good, and nothing is to be rejected if it is received with gratitude.

1 TIMOTHY 4:4 NASB

"We welcome this in every way and everywhere with utmost gratitude."

ACTS 24:3 NRSV

To God be the glory, great things He hath done,
So loved He the world that He gave us His Son,
Who yielded His life an atonement for sin,
And opened the life-gate that all may go in.

"To God Be the Glory," Fanny Crosby

Hearing

May my ears be tuned in to Your voice, Lord! I want to hear Your instruction and Your words of love, not just when I'm overwhelmed but during the comfortable seasons, too. May I always be listening, because I know You're always speaking. Amen.

Apply your heart to discipline and
your ears to words of knowledge.
PROVERBS 23:12 NASB

"Therefore you are great, O LORD God; for there is no one like you, and there is no God besides you, according to all that we have heard with our ears."
2 SAMUEL 7:22 NRSV

"Other seed fell into the good soil, and grew up, and produced a crop a hundred times as great." As He said these things, He would call out, "He who has ears to hear, let him hear."
LUKE 8:8 NASB

Then everyone who has eyes will be able to see the truth, and everyone who has ears will be able to hear it.

ISAIAH 32:3 NLT

Ears to hear and eyes to see—both are gifts from the LORD.

PROVERBS 20:12 NLT

"He who has ears to hear, let him hear."

MATTHEW 11:15 NASB

Lord! give us ears to hear
What Thy good Spirit saith,
With reverence and with godly fear,
With meekness and with faith.

That so, the joyful sound,
Our willing minds may learn,
And, where iniquities abound,
Things excellent discern.

"LORD, GIVE US EARS TO HEAR," JAMES MONTGOMERY

Honesty

Lord, I know how strongly You feel about honesty, and I give it my best shot. Probably the area where I struggle most is in my thought life. I'm not completely honest with myself about how loved I am and how much You love me. I'm also not always honest with You about the things that are troubling me. Would You help me with that? Help me to be honest in every area of my life. Amen.

"Have nothing to do with a false charge and do not put an innocent or honest person to death, for I will not acquit the guilty."

EXODUS 23:7 NIV

You shall have only a full and honest weight; you shall have only a full and honest measure, so that your days may be long in the land that the LORD your God is giving you.

DEUTERONOMY 25:15 NRSV

"Let God weigh me in honest scales and he will know that I am blameless."

JOB 31:6 NIV

He who speaks truth tells what is right,
but a false witness, deceit.
PROVERBS 12:17 NASB

An honest answer is like a kiss on the lips.
PROVERBS 24:26 NIV

"And the seed that fell on the good ground is like those who hear God's teaching with good, honest hearts and obey it and patiently produce good fruit."
LUKE 8:15 NCV

Truthful lips will be established forever,
but a lying tongue is only for a moment.
PROVERBS 12:19 NASB

Guide me in your truth and teach me, for you are God my Savior, and my hope is in you all day long.

Psalm 25:5 NIV

These are the things which you should do: speak the truth to one another; judge with truth and judgment for peace in your gates.

Zechariah 8:16 NASB

So the spies questioned him: "Teacher, we know that you speak and teach what is right, and that you do not show partiality but teach the way of God in accordance with the truth."

Luke 20:21 NIV

The Word became a human and lived among us. We saw his glory—the glory that belongs to the only Son of the Father—and he was full of grace and truth.

John 1:14 NCV

But whoever lives by the truth comes into the light, so that it may be seen plainly that what they have done has been done in the sight of God.

John 3:21 NIV

If high or low our station be,
Of noble or ignoble name;
By uncorrupted honesty,
Thy blessing, Lord, we'll humbly claim.

"If High or Low Our Station Be," Thomas Scott

Injustice

Lord, I must confess I'm not a fan of injustice. I know You aren't, either. Sometimes I want to get angry. Consumed. When those moments come, please remind me that You are a just God and will have Your way. . .in Your time. Amen.

"Do not deny justice to your poor people in their lawsuits."
EXODUS 23:6 NIV

"Be fair in your judging. You must not show special favor to poor people or great people, but be fair when you judge your neighbor."
LEVITICUS 19:15 NCV

"I put on righteousness as my clothing; justice was my robe and my turban."
JOB 29:14 NIV

"I get my knowledge from far away. I'll announce that the God who made me is fair."
JOB 36:3 NIRV

"The Almighty is beyond our reach and exalted in power;
in his justice and great righteousness, he does not oppress."
JOB 37:23 NIV

God is the judge, and even the skies say he is right.
PSALM 50:6 NCV

I know that the LORD will maintain the cause
of the afflicted, and justice for the poor.
PSALM 140:12 NKJV

When you do what is fair, you make godly people glad.
But you terrify those who do what is evil.
PROVERBS 21:15 NIRV

Learn to do good; seek justice, rebuke the oppressor;
defend the fatherless, plead for the widow.
ISAIAH 1:17 NKJV

But let justice roll on like a river,
righteousness like a never-failing stream!

Amos 5:24 NIV

Blessed is the man who walks not in the counsel of the wicked, nor stands in the way of sinners, nor sits in the seat of scoffers; but his delight is in the law of the Lord, and on his law he meditates day and night. He is like a tree planted by streams of water that yields its fruit in its season, and its leaf does not wither. In all that he does, he prospers. The wicked are not so, but are like chaff that the wind drives away. Therefore the wicked will not stand in the judgment, nor sinners in the congregation of the righteous.

Psalm 1:1–5 ESV

But here is what he says about the Son.
"You are God. Your throne will last for ever and ever.
Your kingdom will be ruled by justice."

Hebrews 1:8 NIrV

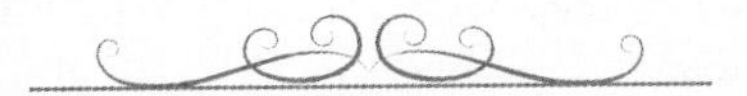

A mighty fortress is our God, a bulwark never failing;
Our helper He, amid the flood of mortal ills prevailing:
For still our ancient foe doth seek to work us woe;
His craft and power are great, and, armed with cruel hate,
On earth is not his equal.

"A Mighty Fortress Is Our God," Martin Luther

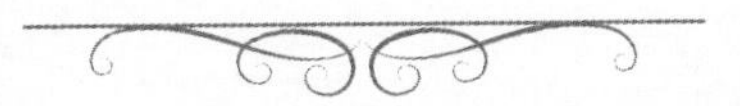

Jesus, God's Son

The ultimate act of sacrifice. That's what You did on my behalf, Father. You sent Your Son—Your only Son, no less—as a sacrifice for my sins. He took the shame and the blame for everything bad that I might ever think or do. How can I begin to thank You for offering Him on my behalf? I'm speechless over such a gift, Lord. And yet, He gave of Himself willingly. "Thank You" doesn't seem like enough, but those are the only words I have. Thank You, Lord. Thank You. Amen.

"Behold, the virgin shall be with child, and bear a Son,
and they shall call His name Immanuel,"
which is translated, "God with us."

MATTHEW 1:23 NKJV

When He had been baptized, Jesus came up immediately from the water; and behold, the heavens were opened to Him, and He saw the Spirit of God descending like a dove and alighting upon Him. And suddenly a voice came from heaven, saying, "This is My beloved Son, in whom I am well pleased."

MATTHEW 3:16–17 NKJV

So Jesus explained, "I tell you the truth, the Son can do nothing by himself. He does only what he sees the Father doing. Whatever the Father does, the Son also does."

JOHN 5:19 NLT

There was a man named Nicodemus, a Jewish religious leader who was a Pharisee. After dark one evening, he came to speak with Jesus. "Rabbi," he said, "we all know that God has sent you to teach us. Your miraculous signs are evidence that God is with you."

Jesus replied, "I tell you the truth, unless you are born again, you cannot see the Kingdom of God."

"What do you mean?" exclaimed Nicodemus. "How can an old man go back into his mother's womb and be born again?"

Jesus replied, "I assure you, no one can enter the Kingdom of God without being born of water and the Spirit."

JOHN 3:1–5 NLT

In the beginning was the Word, and the Word was with God, and the Word was God. He was in the beginning with God. All things were made through Him, and without Him nothing was made that was made. In Him was life, and the life was the light of men. And the light shines in the darkness, and the darkness did not comprehend it.

JOHN 1:1–5 NKJV

Now when evening came, His disciples went down to the sea, and after getting into a boat, they started to cross the sea to Capernaum. It had already become dark, and Jesus had not yet come to them. The sea began to be stirred up because a strong wind was blowing. Then, when they had rowed about three or four miles, they saw Jesus walking on the sea and drawing near to the boat; and they were frightened. But He said to them, "It is I; do not be afraid." So they were willing to receive Him into the boat, and immediately the boat was at the land to which they were going.

John 6:16–21 NASB

The woman said, "I know the Messiah is coming—
the one who is called Christ. When he comes,
he will explain everything to us."
Then Jesus told her, "I AM the Messiah!"

John 4:25-26 NLT

When I survey the wondrous cross
On which the Prince of glory died,
My richest gain I count but loss,
And pour contempt on all my pride.

"When I Survey the Wondrous Cross," Isaac Watts

Joy

Joy unspeakable. That's what You give me, Lord. When I'm down, when I'm hurting, when I'm in distress, You supernaturally cause joy to bubble up inside of me. It's a miracle, really! I change gears immediately—from overwhelmed and confused to blissfully content in You. Praise You for such a gift, Father! Amen.

You will make known to me the path of life; in Your presence is fullness of joy; in Your right hand there are pleasures forever.

Psalm 16:11 NASB

The precepts of the Lord are right, giving joy to the heart. The commands of the Lord are radiant, giving light to the eyes.

Psalm 19:8 NIV

And the disciples were continually filled with joy and with the Holy Spirit.

Acts 13:52 NASB

When anxiety was great within me, your consolation brought me joy.

Psalm 94:19 NIV

"O Lord God, let Your religious leaders be dressed in saving power. Let those who belong to You be filled with joy in what is good."

2 Chronicles 6:41 NLV

Make my joy complete by being of the same mind, maintaining the same love, united in spirit, intent on one purpose.

Philippians 2:2 NASB

But the angel said to them, "Do not be afraid; for behold, I bring you good news of great joy which will be for all the people."

Luke 2:10 NASB

But let all who put their trust in You be glad. Let them sing with joy forever. You make a covering for them, that all who love Your name may be glad in You.

Psalm 5:11 NLV

Sing to him a new song; play skillfully, and shout for joy.
PSALM 33:3 NIV

But I have trusted in Your loving-kindness.
My heart will be full of joy because You will save me.
PSALM 13:5 NLV

"The kingdom of heaven is like a treasure hidden in the field, which a man found and hid again; and from joy over it he goes and sells all that he has and buys that field."
MATTHEW 13:44 NASB

O clap your hands, all peoples;
shout to God with the voice of joy.
PSALM 47:1 NASB

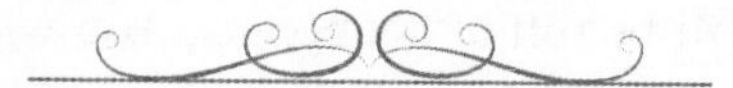

Crown Him with many crowns, the Lamb upon His throne.
Hark! how the heavenly anthem drowns all music but its own!
Awake, my soul, and sing of Him who died for thee,
And hail Him as thy matchless King through all eternity.

"Crown Him with Many Crowns," Matthew Bridges

Judging

You've instructed me to judge not, lest I be judged, Lord. I'll admit, I sometimes forget. But You have a way of reminding me! May I keep my eyes focused on my own behavior, not that of others. I have a sneaking suspicion You're watching them anyway and making all of the necessary correction without my help. Thanks for the reminder that I'm not judge and jury. Amen.

"You judge according to the flesh;
I am not judging anyone."
JOHN 8:15 NASB

"Stop judging only by what you see.
Judge in the right way."
JOHN 7:24 NIRV

For what have I to do with judging outsiders?
Do you not judge those who are within the church?
1 CORINTHIANS 5:12 NASB

If you judge someone else, you have no excuse for it.
When you judge another person, you are judging yourself.
You do the same things you blame others for doing.
ROMANS 2:1 NIRV

You are judging by appearances. If anyone is confident that they belong to Christ, they should consider again that we belong to Christ just as much as they do.

2 Corinthians 10:7 NIV

Let us stop judging one another. Instead, decide not to put anything in the way of a brother or sister. Don't put anything in their way that would make them trip and fall.

Romans 14:13 NIrV

I'm not your judge, nay! God forbids
Me judge the record of your deeds;
But tells me wait, with ready hand,
To love and help and understand;
But tells me wait, with ready hand,
To love, and help, and understand.

Judge not, that ye be not judged;
Judge not, that ye be not judged.

"I'm Not Your Judge," Sarah Spencer Ruff

Keeping Up with the Joneses

Father, I'll admit it. . .sometimes I get overwhelmed just trying to keep up with the people around me. I want what they have. I strive to get things I don't even need. Please help me overcome this temptation, Lord! Amen.

"Why are you sleeping?" [Jesus] asked [his disciples]. "Get up and pray so that you will not fall into temptation."
LUKE 22:46 NIV

What the eyes see is better than what there is a desire for. This also is for nothing, like trying to catch the wind.
ECCLESIASTES 6:9 NLV

"You shall not covet your neighbor's house. You shall not covet your neighbor's wife, or his male or female servant, his ox or donkey, or anything that belongs to your neighbor."
EXODUS 20:17 NIV

"You shall not commit adultery, You shall not murder, You shall not steal, You shall not covet," and if there is any other commandment, it is summed up in this saying, "You shall love your neighbor as yourself."
ROMANS 13:9 NASB

[Joseph's] brothers were jealous of him,
but his father kept the saying in mind.
GENESIS 37:11 NASB

Anger is cruel and fury overwhelming,
but who can stand before jealousy?
PROVERBS 27:4 NIV

Turn your eyes upon Jesus,
Look full in His wonderful face,
And the things of earth will grow strangely dim,
In the light of His glory and grace.
"TURN YOUR EYES UPON JESUS," HELEN LEMMEL

Kindness

It's Your kindness, Lord, that leads me to repentance. Every time. When I blow it, You're right there, kindly ushering me into Your presence to offer grace, mercy, and forgiveness. How could I then not offer kindness to others? I'm doing my best, but often I need a little nudging from You. Bless You for Your kindness toward Your children, Father! Amen.

But the fruit of the Spirit is love, joy, peace, patience, kindness, goodness, faithfulness, gentleness, self-control; against such things there is no law.
GALATIANS 5:22–23 NASB

Then Naomi said to her two daughters-in-law, "Go back, each of you, to your mother's home. May the LORD show you kindness, as you have shown kindness to your dead husbands and to me."
RUTH 1:8 NIV

So, as those who have been chosen of God, holy and beloved, put on a heart of compassion, kindness, humility, gentleness and patience.
COLOSSIANS 3:12 NASB

The LORD appeared to us in the past, saying:
"I have loved you with an everlasting love;
I have drawn you with unfailing kindness."
JEREMIAH 31:3 NIV

Do not let kindness and truth leave you; bind them around your neck, write them on the tablet of your heart.
PROVERBS 3:3 NASB

Do you disrespect God's great kindness and favor? Do you disrespect God when he is patient with you? Don't you realize that God's kindness is meant to turn you away from your sins?
ROMANS 2:4 NIRV

Therefore, as God's chosen people, holy and dearly loved, clothe yourselves with compassion, kindness, humility, gentleness and patience.
COLOSSIANS 3:12 NIV

Fairest Lord Jesus, Ruler of all nature,
O Thou of God and man the Son,
Thee will I cherish, Thee will I honor,
Thou, my soul's glory, joy, and crown.

"Fairest Lord Jesus," Author Unknown

Knowledge

I don't just want to be smart by the world's standards, Lord. I want to have the knowledge that only You can give. Increase my knowledge, I pray. Give me the tools to learn the things that You deem best for my life. Amen.

The LORD God made all kinds of trees grow out of the ground—trees that were pleasing to the eye and good for food. In the middle of the garden were the tree of life and the tree of the knowledge of good and evil.

GENESIS 2:9 NIRV

"Therefore wisdom and knowledge will be given you. And I will also give you wealth, possessions and honor, such as no king who was before you ever had and none after you will have."

2 CHRONICLES 1:12 NIV

"I get my knowledge from far away. I'll announce that the God who made me is fair."

JOB 36:3 NIRV

"But if they do not listen, they will perish
by the sword and die without knowledge."

Job 36:12 NIRV

Teach me knowledge and good judgment,
for I trust your commands.

Psalm 119:66 NIV

The fear of the Lord is the beginning of knowledge,
but fools despise wisdom and instruction.

Proverbs 1:7 NIRV

The one who has knowledge uses words with restraint,
and whoever has understanding is even-tempered.

Proverbs 17:27 NIRV

Those whose hearts understand what is right get knowledge.
That's because the ears of those who are wise listen for it.

Proverbs 18:15 NIRV

"For the earth will be filled with the knowledge of the glory of the LORD as the waters cover the sea."

HABAKKUK 2:14 NIV

He said, "The knowledge of the secrets of the kingdom of God has been given to you, but to others I speak in parables, so that, 'though seeing, they may not see; though hearing, they may not understand.'"

LUKE 8:10 NIV

But thanks be to God, who always leads us as captives in Christ's victory parade. God uses us to spread his knowledge everywhere like a sweet-smelling perfume.

2 CORINTHIANS 2:14 NCV

To the discerning all of them are right; they are upright to those who have found knowledge.

PROVERBS 8:9 NIV

This is my prayer for you: that your love will grow more and more; that you will have knowledge and understanding with your love.

PHILIPPIANS 1:9 NCV

Opponents must be gently instructed, in the hope that God will grant them repentance leading them to a knowledge of the truth.

2 TIMOTHY 2:25 NIV

Grace and peace be yours in abundance through the knowledge of God and of Jesus our Lord.

2 PETER 1:2 NIV

Now for this very reason also, applying all diligence, in your faith supply moral excellence, and in your moral excellence, knowledge.

2 PETER 1:5 NASB

It passeth knowledge, that dear love of Thine,
My Jesus, Savior!—yet this soul of mine
Would of that love, in all its depth and length,
Its height and breadth, and everlasting strength
Know more and more.

"It Passeth Knowledge," Mary Shekleton

Love

Your love, O Lord, sustains me. When I feel as if I can't put one foot in front of the other, I'm propelled—and compelled—by Your love. May I take that love and spread it to others so that they, too, can be strengthened from the inside out. Amen.

Yet the LORD set his affection on your ancestors and loved them, and he chose you, their descendants, above all the nations—as it is today.

DEUTERONOMY 10:15 NIV

"May the LORD your God be praised. He takes great delight in you. He placed you on the throne of Israel. The LORD will love Israel for all time to come. That's why he has made you king. He knows that you will do what is fair and right."

1 KINGS 10:9 NIRV

Give thanks to the LORD,
for he is good; his love endures forever.

PSALM 118:1 NIV

The trumpet players and other musicians played their instruments together. They praised the LORD and gave thanks to him. The singers sang to the music of the trumpets, cymbals and other instruments. The sang in praise to the LORD, "The LORD is good. His faithful love continues forever." Then a cloud filled the temple of the LORD.

2 CHRONICLES 5:13 NIRV

With praise and thanksgiving they sang to the LORD:
"He is good; his love toward Israel endures forever."
And all the people gave a great shout of praise to the LORD,
because the foundation of the house of the LORD was laid.

EZRA 3:11 NIV

But I trust in your unfailing love.
I will rejoice because you have rescued me.

PSALM 13:5 NLT

Show me the wonders of your great love, you who save by your right hand those who take refuge in you from their foes.

PSALM 17:7 NIV

Surely your goodness and love will follow me all the days of my life, and I will dwell in the house of the LORD forever.

PSALM 23:6 NIV

Because Your lovingkindness is better than life, my lips will praise You.

PSALM 63:3 NASB

For I am always aware of your unfailing love, and I have lived according to your truth.

PSALM 26:3 NLT

But I am like an olive tree flourishing in the house of God; I trust in God's unfailing love for ever and ever.

PSALM 52:8 NIV

But as for me, I shall sing of Your strength; yes, I shall joyfully sing of Your lovingkindness in the morning, for You have been my stronghold and a refuge in the day of my distress.

PSALM 59:16 NASB

Let those who fear the LORD say:
"His love endures forever."

PSALM 118:4 NIV

A wonderful Savior is Jesus my Lord,
A wonderful Savior to me;
He hideth my soul in the cleft of the rock,
Where rivers of pleasure I see.

He hideth my soul in the cleft of the rock
That shadows a dry, thirsty land;
He hideth my life in the depths of His love,
And covers me there with His hand,
And covers me there with His hand.

"HE HIDETH MY SOUL," FANNY CROSBY

Loyalty

You're more loyal than the most loyal person I know, Lord. I don't know how or why You've stuck with me this long, especially when I think of the many times I've failed You. But there You are, sticking closer than a brother, nearer than the closest friend I've ever had. I'm so grateful, Father. May I learn to be loyal to You and to others by Your example. Amen.

Help, LORD, for no one is faithful anymore; those who are loyal have vanished from the human race.

PSALM 12:1 NIV

A friend loves at all times, and a brother is born for adversity.

PROVERBS 17:17 ESV

A man of many companions may come to ruin,
but there is a friend who sticks closer than a brother.

PROVERBS 18:24 ESV

Peter said to him, "Even if I must die with you, I will not deny you!" And all the disciples said the same.

MATTHEW 26:35 ESV

Let not steadfast love and faithfulness forsake you; bind them around your neck; write them on the tablet of your heart.

PROVERBS 3:3 ESV

But Ruth said, "Do not urge me to leave you or to return from following you. For where you go I will go, and where you lodge I will lodge. Your people shall be my people, and your God my God. Where you die I will die, and there will I be buried. May the LORD do so to me and more also if anything but death parts me from you."

RUTH 1:16–17 ESV

"If your brother sins against you, go and tell him his fault, between you and him alone. If he listens to you, you have gained your brother."

MATTHEW 18:15 ESV

Iron sharpens iron, and one man sharpens another.

PROVERBS 27:17 ESV

Loyalty to Christ forever joyfully now we sing;
Serving him with true endeavor love we bring;
Yielding full and glad allegiance, following him each day,
Safely with our Captain will we go alway.

"Loyalty!" joyfully now we sing,
Full allegiance give to him forever,
Loyalty unto the Christ our King!
Serving him with true endeavor.

"LOYALTY TO THE KING," LIZZIE DEARMOND

Money

Lord, sometimes money issues stress me out! That's why I'm so glad You own the cattle on a thousand hills. Help me have Your perspective, Father, so that I can be a good steward of all You have entrusted to me. Amen.

For the love of money is a root of all kinds of evil. Some people, eager for money, have wandered from the faith and pierced themselves with many griefs.

1 TIMOTHY 6:10 NIV

He does not put out his money at interest,
nor does he take a bribe against the innocent.
He who does these things will never be shaken.

PSALM 15:5 NASB

Riches taken by false ways become less and less,
but riches grow for the one who gathers by hard work.

PROVERBS 13:11 NLV

Whoever loves money never has enough; whoever loves wealth is never satisfied with their income. This too is meaningless.

ECCLESIASTES 5:10 NIV

"Listen! Every one who is thirsty, come to the waters. And you who have no money, come, buy and eat. Come, buy wine and milk without money and without price."

ISAIAH 55:1 NLV

"Suppose one of you wants to build a tower. Won't you first sit down and estimate the cost to see if you have enough money to complete it?"

LUKE 14:28 NIV

"Why do you spend money for what is not bread, and your wages for what does not satisfy? Listen carefully to Me, and eat what is good, and delight yourself in abundance."

ISAIAH 55:2 NASB

"No one can serve two masters. Either you will hate the one and love the other, or you will be devoted to the one and despise the other. You cannot serve both God and money."

MATTHEW 6:24 NIV

Keep your lives free from the love of money and be content with what you have, because God has said, "Never will I leave you; never will I forsake you."

HEBREWS 13:5 NIV

Take my life and let it be
Consecrated, Lord, to Thee.
Take my moments and my days;
Let them flow in endless praise,
Let them flow in endless praise.

Take my silver and my gold;
Not a mite would I withhold.
Take my intellect and use
Every power as Thou shalt choose,
Every power as Thou shalt choose.

"Take My Life and Let It Be," Frances Havergal

Obedience

I have to keep reminding myself that obedience isn't a dirty word, Lord. So often I just want to go my own way, make my own path. Then I'm reminded—usually through Your Word or the Spirit's nudging—that I've gotten away from Your perfect will for my life. Thanks for reeling me in, Father. It's not easy to obey, but it's always for my benefit. Thanks for that reminder. Amen.

Walk in obedience to all that the LORD your God has commanded you, so that you may live and prosper and prolong your days in the land that you will possess.

DEUTERONOMY 5:33 NIV

Therefore, you shall keep the commandments of the LORD your God, to walk in His ways and to fear Him.

DEUTERONOMY 8:6 NASB

You have declared this day that the LORD is your God and that you will walk in obedience to him, that you will keep his decrees, commands and laws—that you will listen to him.

DEUTERONOMY 26:17 NIV

Blessed are all who fear the LORD,
who walk in obedience to him.
PSALM 128:1 NIV

"Now obey me completely. Keep my covenant.
If you do, then out of all of the nations you will
be my special treasure. The whole earth is mine."
EXODUS 19:5 NIRV

"Only be strong and very courageous; be careful to do
according to all the law which Moses My servant
commanded you; do not turn from it to the right or to
the left, so that you may have success wherever you go."
JOSHUA 1:7 NASB

Oh, that my ways were steadfast in obeying your decrees!
PSALM 119:5 NIV

I will always obey your law, for ever and ever.

Psalm 119:44 NIrV

[Jesus] replied, "Instead, blessed are those who hear God's word and obey it."

Luke 11:28 NIrV

[Jesus] replied, "If you have faith as small as a mustard seed, you can say to this mulberry tree, 'Be uprooted and planted in the sea,' and it will obey you."

Luke 17:6 NIV

"And we are witnesses of these things; and so is the Holy Spirit, whom God has given to those who obey Him."

Acts 5:32 NASB

But if anyone obeys his word, love for God is truly made complete in them. This is how we know we are in him: Whoever claims to live in him must live as Jesus did.

1 John 2:5–6 NIV

When we walk with the Lord in the light of His Word,
What a glory He sheds on our way!
While we do His good will, He abides with us still,
And with all who will trust and obey.

Trust and obey, for there's no other way
To be happy in Jesus, but to trust and obey.

"TRUST AND OBEY," JOHN H. SAMMIS

Patience

I have to confess, I'm not very patient, Lord. I want what I want when I want it. And when You (seemingly) don't come through for me, I often get discouraged or overwhelmed. How ashamed I am when I see Your answer for my issue, for it's usually better than what I would've dreamed for myself. Help me, Father. May my patience grow and grow!

Rather, as servants of God we commend ourselves in every way: in great endurance; in troubles, hardships and distresses; in beatings, imprisonments and riots; in hard work, sleepless nights and hunger; in purity, understanding, patience and kindness; in the Holy Spirit and in sincere love.

2 Corinthians 6:4–6 niv

God will strengthen you with his own great power so that you will not give up when troubles come, but you will be patient.

Colossians 1:11 ncv

Therefore, as God's chosen people, holy and dearly loved, clothe yourselves with compassion, kindness, humility, gentleness and patience.

Colossians 3:12 niv

Be patient, then, brothers and sisters, until the Lord's coming. See how the farmer waits for the land to yield its valuable crop, patiently waiting for the autumn and spring rains.

JAMES 5:7 NIV

You, however, know all about my teaching, my way of life, my purpose, faith, patience, love, endurance, persecutions, sufferings—what kinds of things happened to me in Antioch, Iconium and Lystra, the persecutions I endured. Yet the Lord rescued me from all of them.

2 TIMOTHY 3:10–11 NIV

Be joyful because you have hope. Be patient when trouble comes, and pray at all times.

ROMANS 12:12 NCV

But for that very reason I was shown mercy so that in me, the worst of sinners, Christ Jesus might display his immense patience as an example for those who would believe in him and receive eternal life.

1 TIMOTHY 1:16 NIV

Love is patient, love is kind and is not jealous;
love does not brag and is not arrogant.

1 Corinthians 13:4 NASB

Be completely humble and gentle;
be patient, bearing with one another in love.

Ephesians 4:2 NIV

The Lord is not slow in doing what he promised—the way some people understand slowness. But God is being patient with you. He does not want anyone to be lost, but he wants all people to change their hearts and lives.

2 Peter 3:9 NCV

I need Thee every hour,
Most gracious Lord;
No tender voice like Thine
Can peace afford.

I need Thee, O I need Thee,
Every hour I need Thee!
O bless me now, my Savior,
I come to Thee!

"I Need Thee Every Hour," Annie S. Hawks

Peace

Ah, peace! I'm so grateful for it, Lord. Even when storms are blowing around me, I don't have to be overwhelmed. I can rest in Your peace, knowing You are my shield and protector. Amen.

"I leave my peace with you. I give my peace to you. I do not give it to you as the world does. Do not let your hearts be troubled. And do not be afraid."

John 14:27 NIrV

I pray that the God who gives hope will fill you with much joy and peace while you trust in him. Then your hope will overflow by the power of the Holy Spirit.

Romans 15:13 NCV

"May the Lord look on you with favor and give you peace."

Numbers 6:26 NIrV

But soon you will cross the Jordan River to live in the land the Lord your God is giving you as your own, where he will give you rest from all your enemies and you will live in safety.

Deuteronomy 12:10 NCV

I will listen to what God the Lord says. He promises peace to his faithful people. But they must not turn to foolish ways.

Psalm 85:8 NIRV

"I have told you these things, so that you can have peace because of me. In this world you will have trouble. But be encouraged! I have won the battle over the world."

John 16:33 NIRV

"I praise the Lord. He has given peace and rest to his people Israel. That's exactly what he promised to do. He gave his people good promises through his servant Moses. Every single word of those promises has come true."

1 Kings 8:56 NIRV

He said to her, "Dear woman, your faith has healed you.
Go in peace. You are free from your suffering."

MARK 5:34 NIRV

Sweet peace is flowing, peace that will abide;
Peace e'er increasing, Jesus will provide;
Peace like a river in the time of drouth,
Flowing on forever, from the sunny south.

Peace, peace, wonderful peace!
Flowing so deep in my soul;
Peace, peace, sweet peace,
How it maketh the sad heart whole.

"SWEET PEACE IS FLOWING," BARNEY E. WARREN

Praise

Lord, You are worthy of praise! No matter what I'm going through, no matter how overwhelmed I get, things always look better after I start praising You. Praise lifts my heart and my spirits. Best of all, it puts You in Your rightful place! You are exalted, Father! Praise Your holy name! Amen.

"I called to the LORD, who is worthy of praise,
and have been saved from my enemies."
2 SAMUEL 22:4 NIV

Oh give thanks to the LORD, call upon His name;
make known His deeds among the peoples.
1 CHRONICLES 16:8 NASB

Sing to him, sing praise to him; tell of all his wonderful acts.
1 CHRONICLES 16:9 NIV

When he had consulted with the people, he appointed those who sang to the Lord and those who praised Him in holy attire, as they went out before the army and said, "Give thanks to the Lord, for His lovingkindness is everlasting."

2 Chronicles 20:21 NASB

I will praise the Lord, who counsels me;
even at night my heart instructs me.

Psalm 16:7 NIV

The Lord lives! Praise be to my Rock!
Exalted be God my Savior!

Psalm 18:46 NIV

My foot stands on a level place; in the congregations I shall bless the Lord.

Psalm 26:12 NASB

Sing joyfully to the LORD, you righteous;
it is fitting for the upright to praise him.
PSALM 33:1 NIV

Praise the LORD with the harp; make music
to him on the ten-stringed lyre.
PSALM 33:2 NIV

He put a new song in my mouth, a song of praise to our God;
many will see and fear and will trust in the LORD.
PSALM 40:3 NASB

For what you have done I will always praise you in the
presence of your faithful people. And I will hope
in your name, for your name is good.
PSALM 52:9 NIV

In God, whose word I praise, in God I have put my trust;
I shall not be afraid. What can mere man do to me?

Psalm 56:4 NASB

Praise be to his glorious name forever; may the whole
earth be filled with his glory. Amen and Amen.

Psalm 72:19 NIV

Bless the Lord, O my soul! O LORD my God,
You are very great: You are clothed with honor and majesty.

Psalm 104:1 NKJV

Thank you for making me so wonderfully complex!
Your workmanship is marvelous—how well I know it.

Psalm 139:14 NLT

Sing to the LORD a new song, his praise from the ends of the earth, you who go down to the sea, and all that is in it, you islands, and all who live in them.

ISAIAH 42:10 NIV

The crowd was amazed! Those who hadn't been able to speak were talking, the crippled were made well, the lame were walking, and the blind could see again! And they praised the God of Israel.

MATTHEW 15:31 NLT

They asked Jesus, "Do you hear what these children are saying?" "Yes," Jesus replied. "Haven't you ever read the Scriptures? For they say, 'You have taught children and infants to give you praise.'"

MATTHEW 21:16 NLT

Immediately he received his sight and followed Jesus, praising God. When all the people saw it, they also praised God.

LUKE 18:43 NIV

Accept one another, then, just as Christ accepted you, in order to bring praise to God.

ROMANS 15:7 NIV

Holy, holy, holy! Lord God Almighty!
Early in the morning our song shall rise to Thee.
Holy, holy, holy! Merciful and mighty,
God in three Persons, blessed Trinity!

"HOLY, HOLY, HOLY!" REGINALD HEBER

Prayer

What a privilege, Father, to come into Your presence and place my petitions at Your feet. You listen, You advise, You encourage. Best of all, You truly care and You welcome me, no matter what I've done. Thank You for bearing my burdens during my prayer time, Lord. I'm so grateful for our communication. Amen.

The LORD will command His lovingkindness in the daytime, and in the night His song shall be with me—a prayer to the God of my life.

PSALM 42:8 NKJV

Listen to my prayer for mercy as I cry out to you for help, as I lift my hands toward your holy sanctuary.

PSALM 28:2 NLT

Hear my prayer, O God; give ear to the words of my mouth.

PSALM 54:2 NKJV

Once Jesus was in a certain place praying. As he finished, one of his disciples came to him and said, "Lord, teach us to pray, just as John taught his disciples."

LUKE 11:1 NLT

I have not stopped thanking God for you. I always remember you in my prayers.

EPHESIANS 1:16 NIRV

The LORD is far from the wicked, but He hears the prayer of the righteous.

PROVERBS 15:29 NKJV

So confess your sins to one another. Pray for one another so that you might be healed. The prayer of a godly person is powerful. Things happen because of it.

JAMES 5:16 NIRV

Give a lot of time and effort to prayer.
Always be watchful and thankful.
COLOSSIANS 4:2 NIRV

They all met together and were constantly united
in prayer, along with Mary the mother of Jesus,
several other women, and the brothers of Jesus.
ACTS 1:14 NLT

"And whatever things you ask in prayer,
believing, you will receive."
MATTHEW 21:22 NKJV

Sweet hour of prayer, sweet hour of prayer,
That calls me from a world of care,
And bids me at my Father's throne
Make all my wants and wishes known.
In seasons of distress and grief,
My soul has often found relief,
And oft escaped the tempter's snare
By thy return, sweet hour of prayer!

"Sweet Hour of Prayer," William Walford

Promises

So many people have failed me, Lord, but You never have. Others have made promises and not kept them. If You say it, I can believe it. You've proven Yourself time and time again. I'm so grateful that You are a God who keeps His promises. Praise You for that! Amen.

For no matter how many promises God has made, they are "Yes" in Christ. And so through him the "Amen" is spoken by us to the glory of God.

2 Corinthians 1:20 NIV

The Lord kept all the good promises he had made to the Israelites. Every one of them came true.

Joshua 21:45 NIrV

Then they believed his promises and sang his praise.

Psalm 106:12 NIV

Your kingdom is an everlasting kingdom, and your dominion endures through all generations. The LORD is trustworthy in all he promises and faithful in all he does.

PSALM 145:13 NIV

Now the promises were spoken to Abraham and to his seed. He does not say, "And to seeds," as referring to many, but rather to one, "And to your seed," that is, Christ.

GALATIANS 3:16 NASB

Is the law, therefore, opposed to the promises of God? Absolutely not! For if a law had been given that could impart life, then righteousness would certainly have come by the law.

GALATIANS 3:21 NIV

"Lord, people find the will to live because you keep your promises. And my spirit also finds life in your promises. You brought me back to health. You let me live."

ISAIAH 38:16 NIRV

For by these He has granted to us His precious and magnificent promises, so that by them you may become partakers of the divine nature, having escaped the corruption that is in the world by lust.

2 PETER 1:4 NASB

Standing on the promises of Christ my King,
Through eternal ages let His praises ring;
Glory in the highest, I will shout and sing,
Standing on the promises of God.

Standing, standing,
Standing on the promises of God my Savior;
Standing, standing,
I'm standing on the promises of God.

"STANDING ON THE PROMISES," RUSSELL KELSO CARTER

Purity

You've called me to live a life of purity, Father, and I'm trying! I'm learning that You care as much about my thoughts and the issues in my heart as You do my outward actions. Ouch! Please help me, Lord. It's easier to behave myself externally than to let go of my bitterness, pain, and frustration. I need Your help, Father. Amen.

Let no one despise your youth, but be an example
to the believers in word, in conduct, in love,
in spirit, in faith, in purity.

1 Timothy 4:12 NKJV

Create in me a pure heart, O God,
and renew a steadfast spirit within me.

Psalm 51:10 NIV

God is truly good to Israel. He is good
to those who have pure hearts.

Psalm 73:1 NIRV

All a person's ways seem pure to them,
but motives are weighed by the LORD.

Proverbs 16:2 NIV

"Blessed are the pure in heart, for they will see God."

Matthew 5:8 NIV

Do all things without complaining and disputing, that you may become blameless and harmless, children of God without fault in the midst of a crooked and perverse generation, among whom you shine as lights in the world, holding fast the word of life, so that I may rejoice in the day of Christ that I have not run in vain or labored in vain.

Philippians 2:14–16 NKJV

Finally, brothers and sisters, whatever is true, whatever is noble, whatever is right, whatever is pure, whatever is lovely, whatever is admirable—if anything is excellent or praiseworthy—think about such things.

Philippians 4:8 NIV

So let us come near to God with a sincere heart. Let us come near boldly because of our faith. Our hearts have been sprinkled. Our minds have been cleansed from a sense of guilt. Our bodies have been washed with pure water.

Hebrews 10:22 NIrV

Religion that God our Father accepts as pure and faultless is this: to look after orphans and widows in their distress and to keep oneself from being polluted by the world.

James 1:27 NIV

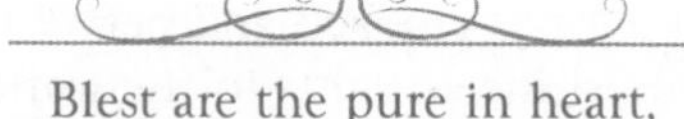

Blest are the pure in heart,
For they shall see our God;
The secret of the Lord is theirs;
Their soul is Christ's abode.

Lord, we Thy presence seek;
Ours may this blessing be;
O give the pure and lowly heart,
A temple meet for Thee.

"Blest Are the Pure in Heart," John Keble

Repentance

You are such a gracious Father! You offer so many chances. I'm so grateful for repentance, Lord. You offer your children the opportunity to confess their sins and to receive forgiveness, and then You turn us around—180 degrees—and put our feet on a new road, one that leads directly to You. How I praise You, Lord! Amen.

"I indeed baptize you with water unto repentance, but He who is coming after me is mightier than I, whose sandals I am not worthy to carry. He will baptize you with the Holy Spirit and fire."

MATTHEW 3:11 NKJV

And so John the Baptist appeared in the wilderness, preaching a baptism of repentance for the forgiveness of sins.

MARK 1:4 NIV

"I have not come to call the righteous, but sinners, to repentance."

LUKE 5:32 NKJV

"So watch yourselves. If your brother or sister sins against you, rebuke them; and if they repent, forgive them."

LUKE 17:3 NIV

The Lord is not slack concerning His promise, as some count slackness, but is longsuffering toward us, not willing that any should perish but that all should come to repentance.

2 PETER 3:9 NKJV

From that time on Jesus began to preach, "Repent, for the kingdom of heaven has come near."

MATTHEW 4:17 NIV

"I say to you that likewise there will be more joy in heaven over one sinner who repents than over ninety-nine just persons who need no repentance."

LUKE 15:7 NKJV

"Produce fruit in keeping with repentance. And do not begin to say to yourselves, 'We have Abraham as our father.' For I tell you that out of these stones God can raise up children for Abraham."

LUKE 3:8 NIV

"Unless you repent you will all likewise perish."

LUKE 13:5 NKJV

"In the same way, I tell you, there is rejoicing in the presence of the angels of God over one sinner who repents."

LUKE 15:10 NIV

"Even if they sin against you seven times in a day and seven times come back to you saying 'I repent,' you must forgive them."

LUKE 17:4 NIV

Peter replied, "Repent and be baptized, every one of you,
in the name of Jesus Christ for the forgiveness of your sins.
And you will receive the gift of the Holy Spirit."

ACTS 2:38 NIV

Search me, O God, and know my heart today;
Try me, O Savior, know my thoughts, I pray.
See if there be some wicked way in me;
Cleanse me from every sin and set me free.

I praise Thee, Lord, for cleansing me from sin;
Fulfill Thy Word and make me pure within.
Fill me with fire where once I burned with shame;
Grant my desire to magnify Thy name.

Lord, take my life and make it wholly Thine;
Fill my poor heart with Thy great love divine.
Take all my will, my passion, self, and pride;
I now surrender, Lord, in me abide.

"SEARCH ME, O GOD," J. EDWIN ORR

Run the Race

I'm running the race, Lord! I get pretty exhausted at times, but I'm still running. And I'm so grateful that You encourage me every step of the way, even when I'm weary. I'll keep on going. . .with Your help. Thank You, Father, for giving me the tenacity to keep running.

I have fought the good fight,
I have finished the race, I have kept the faith.

2 Timothy 4:7 NIV

Therefore, since we are surrounded by such a great cloud of witnesses, let us throw off everything that hinders and the sin that so easily entangles. And let us run with perseverance the race marked out for us.

Hebrews 12:1 NIV

I will pursue your commands,
for you expand my understanding.

Psalm 119:32 NLT

When you walk, your steps will not be stopped.
If you run, you will not trip.

PROVERBS 4:12 NLV

The name of the LORD is a fortified tower;
the righteous run to it and are safe.

PROVERBS 18:10 NIV

But they who wait upon the Lord will get new strength. They will rise up with wings like eagles. They will run and not get tired. They will walk and not become weak.

ISAIAH 40:31 NLV

Do you not know that in a race all the runners run, but only one gets the prize? Run in such a way as to get the prize.

1 CORINTHIANS 9:24 NIV

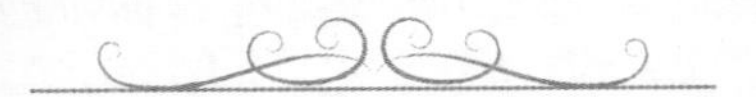

Fight the good fight with all thy might!
Christ is thy strength, and Christ thy right;
Lay hold on life, and it shall be
Thy joy and crown eternally.

Run the straight race through God's good grace,
Lift up thine eyes, and seek His face;
Life with its way before us lies,
Christ is the path, and Christ the prize.

"Fight the Good Fight," J. S. B. Monsell

Shame

Father, I'm glad that You don't heap shame on my head for the many, many times I've failed. Instead of shaming or blaming me, You always choose to forgive. Teach me how to treat others with such grace, Lord. I'm so grateful for Your mercy, Father! Amen.

"Your enemies will be clothed in shame,
and the tents of the wicked will be no more."
Job 8:22 NIV

I trust in you; do not let me be put to shame,
nor let my enemies triumph over me.
Psalm 25:2 NIV

No one who trusts in you will ever be disgraced,
but disgrace comes to those who try to deceive others.
Psalm 25:3 NLT

In you, Lord, I have taken refuge; let me never be put to shame; deliver me in your righteousness.
Psalm 31:1 NIV

But you give us victory over our enemies,
you put our adversaries to shame.
Psalm 44:7 NIV

I will tell about your justice all day long. And those who want to hurt me will be ashamed and disgraced.
Psalm 71:24 NCV

For the Lord God helps Me, therefore, I am not disgraced; therefore, I have set My face like flint, and I know that I will not be ashamed.
Isaiah 50:7 NASB

As the Scriptures tell us, "Anyone who trusts in him will never be disgraced."
ROMANS 10:11 NLT

For this reason I also suffer these things, but I am not ashamed; for I know whom I have believed and I am convinced that He is able to guard what I have entrusted to Him until that day.
2 TIMOTHY 1:12 NASB

For in Scripture it says: "See, I lay a stone in Zion, a chosen and precious cornerstone, and the one who trusts in him will never be put to shame."
1 PETER 2:6 NIV

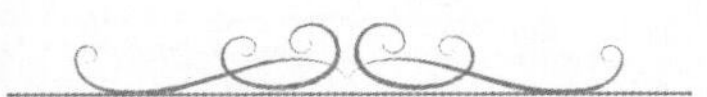

Have you been to Jesus for the cleansing power?
Are you washed in the blood of the Lamb?
Are you fully trusting in His grace this hour?
Are you washed in the blood of the Lamb?

Are you washed in the blood,
In the soul-cleansing blood of the Lamb?
Are your garments spotless? Are they white as snow?
Are you washed in the blood of the Lamb?

"ARE YOU WASHED IN THE BLOOD?" ELISHA HOFFMAN

Sleep

When I'm overwhelmed, I find it hard to sleep, Lord. Please help me to place my head on the pillow, let go of the concerns of the day, and trust You with the details. Grant me sweet sleep, I pray. Amen.

So the LORD God caused him to fall into a deep sleep. While the man was sleeping, the LORD God took out one of the man's ribs. Then the LORD God closed the opening in the man's side.

GENESIS 2:21 NIRV

When he reached a certain place, he stopped for the night because the sun had set. Taking one of the stones there, he put it under his head and lay down to sleep.

GENESIS 28:11 NIV

I lie down and sleep. I wake up again, because the LORD takes care of me.

PSALM 3:5 NIRV

I go to bed and sleep in peace, because,
LORD, only you keep me safe.
PSALM 4:8 NCV

When you lie down, you will not be afraid;
when you lie down, your sleep will be sweet.
PROVERBS 3:24 NIV

After hearing that, I, Jeremiah, woke up and looked around.
My sleep had been very pleasant.
JEREMIAH 31:26 NCV

The sleep of a laborer is sweet, whether they eat little or much,
but as for the rich, their abundance permits them no sleep.
ECCLESIASTES 5:12 NIV

Be not dismayed whate'er betide,
God will take care of you;
Beneath His wings of love abide,
God will take care of you.

God will take care of you,
Through every day, o'er all the way;
He will take care of you,
God will take care of you.

"God Will Take Care of You," Civilla D. Martin

Strength

I like to pretend that I'm strong, Lord, but You know better. On the inside I'm a quivering mess. The only strength in me comes from You, and I'm so grateful for it. Thank You for strengthening me from the inside out. Amen.

"In your unfailing love you will lead the people you have redeemed. In your strength you will guide them to your holy dwelling."
EXODUS 15:13 NIV

You have armed me with strength for the battle; you have subdued my enemies under my feet.
PSALM 18:39 NLT

"Your words have supported those who stumbled; you have strengthened faltering knees."
JOB 4:4 NIV

It is God who arms me with strength and keeps my way secure.
PSALM 18:32 NIV

LORD, you gave me strength to fight the battle.
You made my enemies humble in front of me.

PSALM 18:39 NIRV

The LORD is my strength and my shield; my heart trusts in Him, and I am helped; therefore my heart exults, and with my song I shall thank Him.

PSALM 28:7 NASB

God is our refuge and strength,
always ready to help in times of trouble.

PSALM 46:1 NLT

I pray that out of his glorious riches he may strengthen you with power through his Spirit in your inner being.

EPHESIANS 3:16 NIV

For I can do everything through Christ,
who gives me strength.

PHILIPPIANS 4:13 NLT

And may the Lord cause you to increase and abound in love for one another, and for all people, just as we also do for you; so that He may establish your hearts without blame in holiness before our God and Father at the coming of our Lord Jesus with all His saints.

1 THESSALONIANS 3:12–13 NASB

In a loud voice they were saying: "Worthy is the Lamb, who was slain, to receive power and wealth and wisdom and strength and honor and glory and praise!"

REVELATION 5:12 NIV

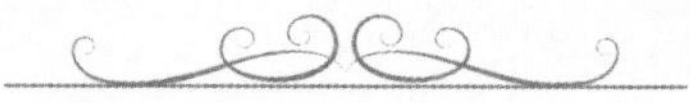

Precious Lord, take my hand,
Lead me on, let me stand,
I am tired, I am weak, I am worn;
Through the storm, through the night,
Lead me on to the light:
Take my hand, precious Lord,
Lead me home.

"PRECIOUS LORD, TAKE MY HAND," THOMAS DORSEY

Temper, Temper!

You see the many times I grit my teeth and threaten to boil over, Lord. Sometimes I do lose it and others witness my temper firsthand. Please forgive me and calm the storm inside, especially during seasons when I'm frustrated or overwhelmed. Only You can truly bring peace, Father, and I'm grateful that You do. Amen.

But you, Lord, are a compassionate and gracious God,
slow to anger, abounding in love and faithfulness.

PSALM 86:15 NIV

Cease from anger and forsake wrath; do not fret;
it leads only to evildoing.

PSALM 37:8 NASB

[Love] does not dishonor others, it is not self-seeking,
it is not easily angered, it keeps no record of wrongs.

1 CORINTHIANS 13:5 NIV

Be angry but do not sin; do not let
the sun go down on your anger.

EPHESIANS 4:26 NRSV

Get rid of all bitterness, rage and anger,
brawling and slander, along with every form of malice.

Ephesians 4:31 NIV

Therefore I want the men in every place to pray,
lifting up holy hands, without wrath and dissension.

1 Timothy 2:8 NASB

For a bishop, as God's steward, must be blameless; he must not be arrogant or quick-tempered or addicted to wine or violent or greedy for gain; but he must be hospitable, a lover of goodness, prudent, upright, devout, and self-controlled.

Titus 1:7–8 NRSV

Do not be quickly provoked in your spirit,
for anger resides in the lap of fools.

Ecclesiastes 7:9 NIV

Teach the older men to be temperate, worthy of respect, self-controlled, and sound in faith, in love and in endurance.

TITUS 2:2 NIV

And we are instructed to turn from godless living and sinful pleasures. We should live in this evil world with wisdom, righteousness, and devotion to God.

TITUS 2:12 NLT

God's will is for you to be holy, so stay away from all sexual sin. Then each of you will control his own body and live in holiness and honor—not in lustful passion like the pagans who do not know God and his ways.

1 THESSALONIANS 4:3–5 NLT

"Give Me thy heart," says the Father above—
No gift so precious to Him as our love;
Softly He whispers wherever thou art,
"Gratefully trust Me and give Me thy heart."

"Give Me thy heart, give Me thy heart"—
Hear the soft whisper, wherever thou art;
From this dark world He would draw thee apart,
Speaking so tenderly, "Give Me thy heart."

"Give Me Thy Heart," Eliza Hewitt

Thankfulness

Oh Lord! I have so much to be thankful for. Sometimes I get overwhelmed by my needs and wants and don't see Your many blessings. Thank You for the reminder that You love me, You bless me, and You continue to pour Yourself out on my behalf. What an awesome God You are, and how thankful I am! Amen.

Let the peace of Christ rule in your hearts, since as members of one body you were called to peace. And be thankful.

COLOSSIANS 3:15 NIV

Give thanks no matter what happens. God wants you to thank him because you believe in Christ Jesus.

1 THESSALONIANS 5:18 NIRV

Devote yourselves to prayer, keeping alert in it with an attitude of thanksgiving.

COLOSSIANS 4:2 NASB

Therefore, since we are receiving a kingdom that cannot be shaken, let us be thankful, and so worship God acceptably with reverence and awe.

HEBREWS 12:28 NIV

Let us worship him with deep respect and wonder.

HEBREWS 12:28 NIRV

Sing to the LORD with grateful praise;
make music to our God on the harp.

PSALM 147:7 NIV

"But I will sacrifice to You with the voice of thanksgiving. That which I have vowed I will pay. Salvation is from the LORD."

JONAH 2:9 NASB

All hail the power of Jesus' name!
Let angels prostrate fall;
Bring forth the royal diadem,
And crown him Lord of all;
Bring forth the royal diadem,
And crown him Lord of all!

"ALL HAIL THE POWER OF JESUS' NAME!" EDWARD PERRONET

Thoughts

Lord, I need help reining in my thoughts. They tend to wander—to my problems, my woes, my lack. You can redirect my thoughts. I know, because You've done it so many times before! Thank You for reminding me through Your Word that You care a great deal about what I'm thinking. I needed that. Amen.

Therefore, holy brothers and sisters, who share in the heavenly calling, fix your thoughts on Jesus, whom we acknowledge as our apostle and high priest.
HEBREWS 3:1 NIV

So let's stop condemning each other. Decide instead to live in such a way that you will not cause another believer to stumble and fall.
ROMANS 14:13 NLT

For the word of God is alive and active. Sharper than any double-edged sword, it penetrates even to dividing soul and spirit, joints and marrow; it judges the thoughts and attitudes of the heart.
HEBREWS 4:12 NIV

Think about things that are in heaven.
Don't think about things that are only on earth.
COLOSSIANS 3:2 NIRV

Do not conform to the pattern of this world,
but be transformed by the renewing of your mind.
Then you will be able to test and approve what
God's will is—his good, pleasing and perfect will.
ROMANS 12:2 NIV

You were taught to be made new in your thinking.
EPHESIANS 4:23 NIRV

In your relationships with one another,
have the same mindset as Christ Jesus.
PHILIPPIANS 2:5 NIV

Then you will experience God's peace, which exceeds anything we can understand. His peace will guard your hearts and minds as you live in Christ Jesus.

PHILIPPIANS 4:7 NLT

Therefore, with minds that are alert and fully sober, set your hope on the grace to be brought to you when Jesus Christ is revealed at his coming.

1 PETER 1:13 NIV

May the mind of Christ, my Savior,
Live in me from day to day,
By His love and power controlling
All I do and say.

May the word of God dwell richly
In my heart from hour to hour,
So that all may see I triumph
Only through His power.

"MAY THE MIND OF CHRIST, MY SAVIOR," KATE WILKINSON

Timing

Timing is everything. That's what I've always heard, anyway. But when I'm waiting on You, Lord. . .sometimes I start to wonder if You've got my best interest at heart. I know You do, but in the moment doubts arise. Thank You for Your reminder in the Word that You're never late or early. You're always right on time. Thank You for that! Amen.

Wait for the LORD; be strong, and let your
heart take courage; wait for the LORD!

PSALM 27:14 ESV

For everything there is a season,
and a time for every matter under heaven.

ECCLESIASTES 3:1 ESV

But do not overlook this one fact, beloved,
that with the Lord one day is as a thousand years,
and a thousand years as one day.

2 PETER 3:8 ESV

Trust in the Lord with all your heart, and do not lean on your own understanding. In all your ways acknowledge him, and he will make straight your paths.

Proverbs 3:5–6 ESV

My times are in your hand; rescue me from the hand of my enemies and from my persecutors!

Psalm 31:15 ESV

He said to them, "It is not for you to know times or seasons that the Father has fixed by his own authority."

Acts 1:7 ESV

For still the vision awaits its appointed time; it hastens to the end—it will not lie. If it seems slow, wait for it; it will surely come; it will not delay.

Habakkuk 2:3 ESV

When morning gilds the skies,
Our hearts awaking cry:
May Jesus Christ be praised!
In all our work and prayer
We ask His loving care:
May Jesus Christ be praised!

To God, the Word on high,
The hosts of angels cry:
May Jesus Christ be praised!
Let mortals too upraise
Their voices in hymns of praise:
May Jesus Christ be praised!

"WHEN MORNING GILDS THE SKIES," TRANSLATED BY EDWARD CASWALL

Trust

I'm learning to trust You, Lord. It's not always easy. Sometimes I get distracted by the circumstances around me. They're just a diversion, I know. You are the only One who is trustworthy, so I recommit myself to trusting You, even when it seems to make no sense. Help me with this, I pray. Amen.

Those who know your name trust in you, for you, LORD, have never forsaken those who seek you.

PSALM 9:10 NIV

But I trust in your unfailing love;
my heart rejoices in your salvation.

PSALM 13:5 NIV

Yet You are He who brought me forth from the womb;
You made me trust when upon my mother's breasts.

PSALM 22:9 NASB

In God I trust and am not afraid.
What can man do to me?

PSALM 56:11 NIV

He put a new song in my mouth, a song of praise to our God;
many will see and fear and will trust in the LORD.

PSALM 40:3 NASB

You who live in the shelter of the Most High, who abide
in the shadow of the Almighty, will say to the LORD,
"My refuge and my fortress; my God, in whom I trust."

PSALM 91:1–2 NRSV

May the God of hope fill you with all joy and peace
as you trust in him, so that you may overflow with
hope by the power of the Holy Spirit.

ROMANS 15:13 NIV

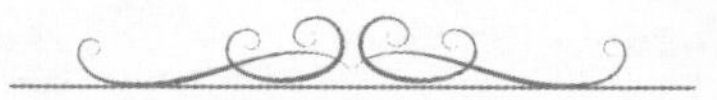

'Tis so sweet to trust in Jesus,
Just to take Him at His word;
Just to rest upon His promise,
Just to know, "Thus saith the Lord!"

Jesus, Jesus, how I trust Him!
How I've proved Him o'er and o'er;
Jesus, Jesus, precious Jesus!
Oh, for grace to trust Him more!

"'TIS SO SWEET TO TRUST IN JESUS," LOUISA M. R. STEAD

Wisdom

I'm learning, Lord! There's a difference between worldly knowledge and godly wisdom. Knowledge is good, but wisdom that flows from Your heart is even better. Draw me close so that I can learn from You, Father. I want the wisdom that only You can give. Amen.

"Wisdom and power belong to God.
Advice and understanding also belong to him."
JOB 12:13 NIRV

"Do you listen in on God's council?
Do you have a monopoly on wisdom?"
JOB 15:8 NIV

"What advice you have offered to one without wisdom!
And what great insight you have displayed!"
JOB 26:3 NIV

My mouth will speak wisdom, and the meditation
of my heart will be understanding.
PSALM 49:3 NASB

"But where can wisdom be found?
Where does understanding dwell?"
JOB 28:12 NIV

"Don't bother to talk about coral and jasper.
Wisdom is worth far more than rubies."
JOB 28:18 NIRV

"And he said to the human race, 'The fear of the Lord—
that is wisdom, and to shun evil is understanding.'"
JOB 28:28 NIV

"Is not wisdom found among the aged?
Does not long life bring understanding?"
JOB 12:12 NIV

Behold, You desire truth in the innermost being,
and in the hidden part You will make me know wisdom.
PSALM 51:6 NASB

The fear of the LORD is the beginning of wisdom;
all who follow his precepts have good understanding.
To him belongs eternal praise.
PSALM 111:10 NIV

Wisdom shouts in the street,
she lifts her voice in the square.
PROVERBS 1:20 NASB

Do not forsake wisdom, and she will protect you;
love her, and she will watch over you.
PROVERBS 4:6 NIV

"I am wisdom, and I have good judgment.
I also have knowledge and good sense."
PROVERBS 8:12 NCV

"To God belong wisdom and power;
counsel and understanding are his."
JOB 12:13 NIV

"If only you would be altogether silent!
For you, that would be wisdom."
JOB 13:5 NIV

Doing wickedness is like sport to a fool,
and so is wisdom to a man of understanding.
PROVERBS 10:23 NASB

How great the wisdom, power, and grace,
Which in redemption shine!
The heavenly host with joy confess
The work is all divine.

Before His feet they cast their crowns,
Those crowns which Jesus gave,
And, with ten thousand tongues,
Proclaim His power to save.

They tell the triumphs of His cross,
The sufferings which He bore;
How low He stooped, how high He rose,
And rose to stoop no more.

With them let us our voices raise,
And still the song renew;
Salvation well deserves the praise
Of men, and angels, too.

"How Great the Wisdom," Benjamin Beddome

Witnesses

You've called us to be witnesses, Lord, to share the good news of the Gospel with those around us. I try, but I'm not always the best witness. Help me, Father. I need Your unction to care more, to try harder, and to garner the courage to speak when You move me to speak. I give myself to this task once more. Use me, I pray. Amen.

"But you will receive power when the Holy Spirit comes on you; and you will be my witnesses in Jerusalem, and in all Judea and Samaria, and to the ends of the earth."

ACTS 1:8 NIV

He came as a witness to testify to the light, so that all might believe through him.

JOHN 1:7 NRSV

"We have seen these things and are telling about them. The Holy Spirit makes these things known also. God gives His Spirit to those who obey Him."

ACTS 5:32 NLV

Fight the good fight of the faith; take hold of the eternal life, to which you were called and for which you made the good confession in the presence of many witnesses.

1 TIMOTHY 6:12 NRSV

Therefore, since we are surrounded by such a great cloud of witnesses, let us throw off everything that hinders and the sin that so easily entangles. And let us run with perseverance the race marked out for us.

HEBREWS 12:1 NIV

You are witnesses, and God also, how pure, upright, and blameless our conduct was toward you believers.

1 THESSALONIANS 2:10 NRSV

An honest witness tells the truth,
but a false witness tells lies.

PROVERBS 12:17 NIV

"You can speak for Me," says the Lord. "You are My servant whom I have chosen so that you may know and believe Me, and understand that I am He. No God was made before Me, and there will be none after Me."

Isaiah 43:10 NLV

"Do not tremble, do not be afraid. Did I not proclaim this and foretell it long ago? You are my witnesses. Is there any God besides me? No, there is no other Rock; I know not one."

Isaiah 44:8 NIV

I love to tell the story of unseen things above,
Of Jesus and His glory, of Jesus and His love.
I love to tell the story, because I know 'tis true;
It satisfies my longings as nothing else can do.

I love to tell the story,
'Twill be my theme in glory,
To tell the old, old story
Of Jesus and His love.

"I Love to Tell the Story," A. Katherine Hankey

Words

Our words are so important, Father! I'm learning when to speak and when not to. I don't always get it right, but I'm trying. I'm also learning that negative words impact my thoughts, so I'm doing my best to keep it positive—with Your help, of course! Thanks for the reminder that words matter. Amen.

We show we are servants of God by our pure lives, our understanding, patience, and kindness, by the Holy Spirit, by true love, by speaking the truth, and by God's power. We use our right living to defend ourselves against everything.

2 Corinthians 6:6–7 NCV

But since you excel in everything—in faith, in speech, in knowledge, in complete earnestness and in the love we have kindled in you—see that you also excel in this grace of giving.

2 Corinthians 8:7 NIV

Don't let anyone look down on you because you are young. Set an example for the believers in what you say and in how you live. Also set an example in how you love and in what you believe. Show the believers how to be pure.

1 Timothy 4:12 NIrV

"Whoever would love life and see good days must keep their tongue from evil and their lips from deceitful speech."

1 Peter 3:10 NIV

Don't let any evil talk come out of your mouths. Say only what will help to build others up and meet their needs. Then what you say will help those who listen.

Ephesians 4:29 NIrV

Do not be quick with your mouth, do not be hasty in your heart to utter anything before God. God is in heaven and you are on earth, so let your words be few.

Ecclesiastes 5:2 NIV

"I have put My words in your mouth, and have covered you with the shadow of My hand. I spread out the heavens and put the earth in its place, and say to Zion, 'You are My people.'"

Isaiah 51:16 NLV

"You must obey God's law about the Sabbath and not do what pleases yourselves on that holy day. You should call the Sabbath a joyful day and honor it as the LORD's holy day. You should honor it by not doing whatever you please nor saying whatever you please on that day."

ISAIAH 58:13 NCV

"As for me, this is my covenant with them," says the LORD. "My Spirit, who is on you, will not depart from you, and my words that I have put in your mouth will always be on your lips, on the lips of your children and on the lips of their descendants—from this time on and forever," says the LORD.

ISAIAH 59:21 NIV

Then the LORD reached out his hand and touched my mouth and said to me, "I have put my words in your mouth."

JEREMIAH 1:9 NIV

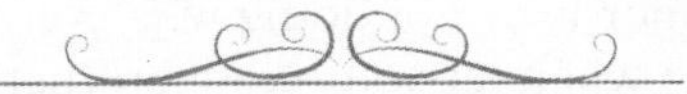

Let Your arms enfold me:
Those who try to wound me
Cannot reach me here.
Though the earth be shaking,
Every heart be quaking,
Jesus calms my fear.
Fires may flash and thunder crash;
Yea, though sin and hell assail me,
Jesus will not fail me.

"Jesus, Priceless Treasure," Johann Franck,
Translated by Catherine Winkworth

Work

I'm a hard worker, Lord! Sometimes I work so hard that I wear myself out. Please help me fulfill my obligations and be a good steward of my time, I pray. When I think I can't go on, give me supernatural strength to get the work done. May I work as unto You in all I do. Amen.

You will enjoy the fruit of your labor.
How joyful and prosperous you will be!
PSALM 128:2 NLT

Whatever my eyes desired I did not keep from them;
I kept my heart from no pleasure, for my heart found pleasure
in all my toil, and this was my reward for all my toil.
ECCLESIASTES 2:10 NRSV

"I sent you to reap what you have not worked for.
Others have done the hard work, and you have
reaped the benefits of their labor."
JOHN 4:38 NIV

The one who plants and the one who waters have a common purpose, and each will receive wages according to the labor of each.
1 CORINTHIANS 3:8 NRSV

"But you, take courage! Do not let your hands be weak, for your work shall be rewarded."
2 CHRONICLES 15:7 NRSV

All hard work brings a profit, but mere talk leads only to poverty.
PROVERBS 14:23 NIV

As we pray to our God and Father about you, we think of your faithful work, your loving deeds, and the enduring hope you have because of our Lord Jesus Christ.
1 THESSALONIANS 1:3 NLT

Then God blessed the seventh day and made it holy, because on it he rested from all the work of creating that he had done.
GENESIS 2:3 NIV

"Bless all his skills, LORD, and be pleased with the work of his hands. Strike down those who rise against him, his foes till they rise no more."
DEUTERONOMY 33:11 NIV

And may the Lord our God show us his approval and make our efforts successful. Yes, make our efforts successful!
PSALM 90:17 NLT

Those who work their land will have abundant food, but those who chase fantasies have no sense.
PROVERBS 12:11 NIV

I have seen that nothing is better than that man should be happy in his activities, for that is his lot. For who will bring him to see what will occur after him?

ECCLESIASTES 3:22 NASB

He told them, "The harvest is plentiful, but the workers are few. Ask the Lord of the harvest, therefore, to send out workers into his harvest field."

LUKE 10:2 NIV

"We must work the works of Him who sent Me as long as it is day; night is coming when no one can work."

JOHN 9:4 NASB

"Stay there, eating and drinking whatever they give you, for the worker deserves his wages. Do not move around from house to house."

LUKE 10:7 NIV

Work, for the night is coming,
Work through the morning hours;
Work while the dew is sparkling,
Work 'mid springing flowers;
Work when the day grows brighter,
Work in the glowing sun;
Work, for the night is coming,
When man's work is done.

Work, for the night is coming,
Work through the sunny noon;
Fill brightest hours with labor,
Rest comes sure and soon.
Give every flying minute
Something to keep in store;
Work, for the night is coming,
When man works no more.

Work, for the night is coming,
Under the sunset skies;
While their bright tints are glowing,
Work, for daylight flies.
Work till the last beam fadeth,
Fadeth to shine no more;
Work, while the night is darkening,
When man's work is o'er.

"Work, for the Night Is Coming," Annie Coghill